Advance Praise for **Black STILL Matters in Marketing**

You won't want to stop reading this book. Successful marketing in the 21st century must go beyond what we used to call the mainstream. Toward the end, Pepper uses the phrase "cultural nuance," and that captures the spirit of this book. Her insights give marketers a fresh understanding of events all around us. I used *What's Black About It?* in my multicultural and ethnic marketing course, but I'm switching—gladly—to *Black Still Matters*.

> JEFF KULICK
> *professor, George Mason University*

What has been created here is the B-school business case. No 21st century marketer can be taken seriously as business leader, driven to bottom-line results, without having read this book. **It is required reading.**

> GWEN KELLY
> *veteran Fortune 500 corporate marketing executive*

Excellent explication and presentation of why Black Matters. Very readable; plain spoken enough that the reader "gets" the meaning without needing SME (subject matter expert) understanding or a familiarity with the terms.

> MARQUIS MILLER
> *Vice President of Field Operations, National Minority Supplier Development Council*

If *What's Black About It?* was the old testament of must have books on African-American marketing, *Black Still Matters in Marketing* is the new. If you are at all interested in marketing to African Americans both these books should be your bibles. *Black Still Matters in Marketing* educates us to why Black marketing still matters in this ever-changing digital world. Blacks are indeed changing, and **this book keeps a close eye on why, how, and what smart marketers can do to capitalize on this still very lucrative market.**

> JIM GLOVER
> *author, Mad Man; VP Executive Creative Director, Actwo Agency*

I loved it! It is unapologetic and a manifesto at the same time. **It is ruthless in taking on each raggedy roadblock and obliterating it with a laser beam of fact and logic.**

> LARRY D. WOODARD
> *President, Graham Stanley Advertising*

Pepper has done it again. **This book captures the essence of Black marketing perspectives in modern day America in an insightful and straight-to-the-point fashion.** This book is a must read for businesses who want to really talk with and to Black America.

GERRY FERNANDEZ
President, Multicultural Foodservice & Hospitality Alliance

Pepper Miller—never one to be outdone—has outdone herself and her wonderful work, *What's Black About It?* with her new book *Black STILL Matters in Marketing.* **Her experience in the African-American marketing arena is without comparison** and *Black STILL Matters* reflects her knowledge and wisdom of the "new Black" in abundance. Pepper, you have done it again!

DAVID R. MORSE
President and CEO, New American Dimensions, LLC

Pepper Miller is a respected marketing professional who has always been at the forefront of progressive thought on the topic of marketing to African Americans. **This book is an invaluable contribution, not only to marketers, but to everyone who wants to better understand the dynamics of the African American community.**

YVETTE MOYO-GILLARD
Founder, Real Men Cook and Real Men Charities

Pepper Miller once again leads marketers to where the money is. As I witness CMO's increased interest in target marketing as a valuable business strategy, this book is timely.

ANDREA HOFFMAN
CEO, Diversity Affluence; co-author, Black is the New Green:
Marketing to Affluent African Americans

Beyond quotes and statistics, *Black Still Matters* peels back the layers of not only Black American buying habits, but also the layers of our culture, our thoughts and motivations.

The conversation is clear and concise—not a wasted page. Beyond it's industry significance, I found *Black Still Matters* to be the tour guide beyond the part of my Black America that is my little world. Yes, you met your objective and greatly increased my cultural IQ.

DONNA SMITH BELLINGER
Outcomes Specialist, GroupEndeavors.com

Black STILL Matters in Marketing

Why Increasing Your Cultural IQ about Black America Is Critical to Your Business and Your Brand

Pepper Miller

Paramount Market Publishing, Inc.

Paramount Market Publishing, Inc.
950 Danby Road, Suite 136, Ithaca, NY 14850
www.paramountbooks.com
Voice: 607-275-8100; 888-787-8100 | Fax: 607-275-8101

Publisher: James Madden
Editorial Director: Doris Walsh

Summertime

Words and Music by Willard Smith, Lamar Mahone, Craig Simpkins, Robert Bell, Ronald Bell, Robert Mickens, Dennis Thomas, George Brown, Alton Taylor, Richard Westfield and Claydus Smith
Copyright © 1991 by Jazzy Jeff And Fresh Prince, Da Posse Music, Warner-Tamerlane Publishing Corp., Second Decade Music Co. and Gang Music Ltd.
All Rights for Jazzy Jeff And Fresh Prince Administered by Universal Music - Z Tunes LLC
All Rights for Da Posse Music Administered by Universal Music - Z Tunes LLC
All Rights for Second Decade Music Co. and Gang Music Ltd. Administered by Warner-Tamerlane Publishing Corp.
International Copyright Secured   All Rights Reserved
- contains samples from "Summer Madness" by Alton Taylor, Robert Mickens, George Brown, Richard Westfield, Claydes Smith, Ronald Bell, Dennis Thomas and Robert Bell
Reprint by Permission of Hal Leonard Corporation

Versions of chapters 3, 14, and 15 were previously published as contributions to *Advertising Age*'s The Big Tent (AdAge.com/bigtent).

This publication is designed to provide accurate and authoritative information in regard to the subject matter covered. It is sold with the understanding that the publisher is not engaged in rendering legal, accounting, or other professional services. If legal advice or other expert assistance is required, the services of a competent professional should be sought.

Library of Congress Catalog available
Cataloging in Publication Data available
ISBN 10: 0-9819869-5-1
ISBN 13: 978-0-9819869-5-1

My BFF.

I miss you.

I miss your big presence: the immensity of your mind and wit—so smart, so funny.

I miss your laugh—so loud and infectious.

I miss seeing you always, always stylish and sharp—so Armani.

I miss our conversations and debates. I miss learning from you and hearing your perspectives about marketing—and particularly the Black consumer—so passionate.

I miss us.

Your wonderful spirit and brilliant contributions are the legacy to all who knew you and to the marketing and advertising industries.

Contents

Acknowledgements ix

Introduction: The New Black xi

Chapter 1 The Profitable "Invisible Middle" 1

Chapter 2 The Dynamics of Black Consumer Marketing 4

Chapter 3 Black America Today: It's STILL A Different World 31

Chapter 4 Black Gold: Finding the Mother Lode Hidden in Plain Sight 52

Chapter 5 Another Opportunity: Wellness Matters 72

Chapter 6 Under the Radar: Black Immigrants and Black Biracials 80
by J.P. James

Chapter 7 Under the Radar: The Black LGBT Community 101
by Reginald Osborne

Chapter 8 Under the Radar: Black Men 106

Chapter 9 Under the Radar: Black Baby Boomers 115

Chapter 10 Under the Radar: Black Women 122
by Sarah Lattimer

Chapter 11 Under the Radar: Blacks and the Green Movement 130

Chapter 12 Making a Connection 133

Chapter 13 Black Media Matter: Old Rules Don't Apply 148
by Pepper Miller with Kevin Walker

Chapter 14 Research Must Be Relevant 182

Chapter 15 Blacks in Advertising Matter 185

Chapter 16 Why Black STILL Matters 192

About the Author and Contributors 201

Index 207

Acknowledgements

For Ron: My sweetheart and my rock. Thank you for being strong, kind and real; for being there when it counts, and for encouraging me to use TRUTH as a platform for change.

Special Thanks to:

Derek Walker of Brown and Browner Advertising: Big D!! Thank you, thank you for encouraging me to tell stories and for helping me tell the story about the value and cultural influence of Black America. You are a wonderful editor and beautiful writer.

John Parikhal: Your support, immeasurable wisdom, mentoring, partnership and friendship means so much.

Executive Coach Linda Cohen: For the relentless ideas and the years of incredible support. I have benefited so much from your contributions and your friendship.

Karyn Pettigrew: My "Zen" coach. Thanks for helping me get unstuck, for working with me on the revamped outline, and for reminding me to embrace the power within.

Contributors Reginald Osborne, Sarah Lattimer, Kevin Walker, J.P. James, and Howard Buford: Thanks so much for taking the time to add your point of view to this work. It means a lot to this industry and me.

x   Black STILL Matters in Marketing

Editorial support and research: C. Gwendolyn Downing—my "sister" from back in the day. Your research and contributions are invaluable. Gwennie, thanks for showin' up and steppin' up. Ashley Jackson, Opal Freeman, Mariscia Thomas and Jacklynn Topping, thanks so much for your research and presenting information on this often difficult subject matter, and to Brandon Yusuf Toropov for editorial support.

My former executive assistant Angie Powell for taking care of The Hunter-Miller Group and me during this process.

JoAnn (Jo) Jackson, my personal trainer: I swear—I might not be alive without your help. The stress of writing a book, maintaining a business and managing life in general was, at times, over the top. And though I b**ched about all those squats, planks and intervals, know that I am grateful for your positive contributions to my overall health. You are a wonderful, knowledgeable trainer, and good friend.

Hattie Jones (Ms. Hattie): For taking exceptional care of my dad. It was comforting to know that he was in good hands while I worked to complete this book.

Paramount Market Publishing, Jim Madden and Doris Walsh, who, with this effort, stood by me, and truly redefined patience.

Introduction: The New Black

A genuine leader is not a searcher for consensus, but a molder of
consensus.
—Martin Luther King, Jr.

Not long ago, Alexander Robinson, a student at Jackson State University, and also the president of the school's chapter of the American Marketing Association, sent me email. He wrote:

> After browsing your website, I read the section concerning the "Mask," similar to W.E.B. Dubois's "Veil." This leads me to ask—should I be pursuing a mission of leading more African Americans into the field of marketing? Or should I be developing aspiring young minds, by removing the whole racial context?
>
> Is Black consumer behavior much different from Whites? Is it now time to stop labeling, and perhaps limiting ourselves with race?

Alexander is not the first to question my Black-American focus and challenge my company's reason for being. When writing about Black America for *Advertising Age*'s multicultural blog, The Big Tent, a few readers accused me of fostering separatism. Yet I continue to respect-fully disagree.

When I launched my company in 1985, I wasn't focused on African Americans. I just wanted to do research to understand what makes people tick. However, when I arrived for my in-person appointment with a consumer goods company I was told, "we don't have any African-

American projects. When we move toward that direction we'll call you."
After enough of those responses and a portfolio that contained only Black
consumer research projects, I decided to embrace the segment—to be the
Black consumer expert. Since that revelation and the gaps in knowledge
that many corporations (and society) have about Black America, The
Hunter-Miller Group's mission has been to:

> "Help corporations and organizations develop a deeper contextual
> understanding of Black-American consumers. This learning will pro-
> vide corporations with the tools needed to create powerful, relevant
> and engaging messages."

Thus, my objective is to bring people together and help them increase
their cultural IQ by providing real (as opposed to invented) insights
with respect to Black America. I'm passionate about our mission, but
I'm no separatist. And that's what I told Alexander. Everything we do,
everything, including this book, is an extension of the Hunter-Miller
Group mission.

Within the five-plus years, since I co-authored *What's Black About It?*
with the late Herb Kemp (2005), much has changed in America. YouTube
launched earlier that year, but there was no social media explosion. Facebook, Twitter, Flickr and Constant Contact didn't exist. Neither did the
iPhone, Droid, or iPad. And there was no President Barack Obama.

Obviously the landscape is altered. Yet despite several major studies
that explored the changing Black American population, there has been
little discussion among marketers about the studies' results and conclu-
sions, and few meaningful discussions about how marketers can better
speak to Black Americans.

- Black Americans have never been a monolith, but they have never
  been more diverse than they are today.

- Since the election of Barack Obama, the country seems more
  socially and racially polarized than ever.

- The Civil Rights Movement continues to be a dividing line between two mindsets: those who fought for it and those who take it for granted.

- Black Americans are making huge strides in education, politics and business, while balancing their desire to stay connected with Black identity and Black culture.
- Black Millennials reject the traditional definition of "Black." "Black" doesn't totally define them. Most are all about being open and inclusive, yet many still want to congregate in spaces where there are other Black people like them.
- Additionally, as Millennials age and experience the "real world," many are re-evaluating their perceptions about race relations in America and re-examining the relationship between their identity and culture with the idea of being successful.
- The definition of the Black family is changing: Seventy-three percent of all Black births are to single moms.
- At the same time, being a single Black mom no longer means you are a "bad mom."
- More Black men are focusing on the importance of good role modeling and being more involved fathers.
- The Digital Divide is finally diminishing, as Blacks are catching up with Caucasians in online access and surpassing them in mobile computing.
- There are countless successful new media platforms created by Blacks for Blacks in support of the strong and powerful Black social network and Black blogosphere, yet when marketers consider complex dynamics like these, they find themselves facing a wealth of opportunities and one impossible-to-ignore conclusion:

Black still matters.

I talked with Alexander for over an hour. I shared these thoughts with him, sent him some of my articles, and directed him toward some relevant websites and blogs (such as *Advertising Age*'s The Big Tent). I also asked him to read some particularly eloquent posts by Tim Wise, an American anti-racist activist and author who, as a White male, writes passionately and prophetically about equality, race, and social justice. A few days later, Alexander sent me this email message:

> Thank you, Pepper. I had not realized how much sociological ideas played into marketing. I read your blog as well as some of the commentary by Tim Wise. This is something that I believe all of my peers and classmates should know about.

This book is not about "targeting" as much as it is about attempting to help move the marketing conversation forward to show what the history, emotions, insights and findings really mean. In *Black STILL Matters in Marketing*, I offer frank talk about solutions that will help marketers better understand, and speak more comfortably with Black America.

Why This subject? Why Now?

Because now is the right time.

Marketers are fighting for their survival—companies are downsizing, merging or being acquired at a phenomenal rate; the economy has slowed; and the number of competitors has increased in many market segments. The pace of doing business has increased to an unimaginable speed with the growth of the internet; to say marketers are busy is an understatement. Many marketers have seen their workloads and responsibilities double, even triple while they're given less time to think. It is a struggle to keep up with current markets, let alone learn and understand ever growing and evolving multicultural segments.

It is easy to understand how marketers can mistakenly accept the myth within each multicultural market segment that all Blacks are the same, all Latinos are the same, and all Asians are the same. This isn't done out of disrespect as much as from a lack of understanding of the people that make up each segment. It is easier and feels more politically correct to adopt myths such as, "We are all alike," or, as in the case of Tim and Cathy (*See* The Post-Racial Mindset, *page 11*) who embrace the belief that "people are people." It is easy to see how a single umbrella strategy for all segments is preferred.

Marketers are not completely in the dark when it comes to the issue of multicultural marketing. According to a 2008 study for the search firm Heidrick & Struggles, conducted by Brandiosity, 84 percent of marketers believe multicultural marketing is "critical to my business." Yet, almost 40 percent said they don't know the financial value of multicultural groups to their companies.

Carla Palazio, a partner at Heidrick & Struggles, said the recruiting firm commissioned the study to discover what companies needed to target multicultural segments—particularly what sort of talent they were looking for and specifically through the eyes of the CMO. The study found a disconnect. Many CMOs recognize the importance of multicultural marketing, but many companies still lack a real company-wide strategy to address it.

"The root of this is the lack of awareness in the organization. While the CMO understands it well, he or she almost has to evangelize [the value of multicultural marketing] to the rest of the company," Ms. Palazio said.[1]

There's no quick or easy fix to this issue. We can't wave a wand and make everything work; it is going to take better understanding and exposure to multicultural segments. Marketers are going to have to find the time to create a strategy that includes multicultural marketing and identify the people to execute the strategy.

As marketers create strategies that include multicultural segments there's another issue or hurdle they will have to clear—not knowing the customers.

Marketers have to understand that they cannot judge customers for being different from them or by some idealistic standard that does not represent real customers. Instead marketers are going to have to get to know these segments individually, see them for who they really are, and learn their experiences and needs. This is a real opportunity to forge deep and lasting relationships with groups of customers who have been overlooked and unengaged.

Real insights are more than light bulb moments. They are gleaned from opening up to people and situations that are completely different from our own. Experience is still the best teacher—more than reading or hearing about something.

Sometimes we have to embrace being uncomfortable to become comfortable with one another. I learned this with my first intern. I was open to working with him but I have to admit, I was also a bit little leery.

"How is a person who just landed from China (literally) albeit an MBA candidate, with good English language and computer skills going to work on Black consumer trends?" I asked myself.

Thankfully my apprehension quickly faded after our first conversation. We were both excited. We immediately began to talk about cultural differences (with interest). I shared examples of Black nuances that helped shape successful marketing campaigns, and he shared his experiences with Black acquaintances. Later he told me that he had questions that he wanted to ask of his acquaintances (to get to know them better and understand the culture) but was afraid of being labeled insensitive, stupid, or a racist.

Sometimes, we are the creators of the "class system" that we despise. We refuse to walk in others' shoes, to attempt to see the world through their eyes. Instead, we try to force people to be more like us, to think like us. It is not something done maliciously. Many don't even realize what they are doing.

I've worked with a couple of clients who had products that were targeted to mid-to-lower-income customers. In those cases, African Americans represented a significant percentage of their businesses. We talked with this segment in focus groups and one-on-one interviews to learn about their needs, and when the customers spoke in their colloquial language and told stories about their lifestyle that didn't fit with the clients' upscale attitudes, the client was turned off.

These marketers proceeded to craft marketing and advertising that totally ignored the language, stories, and lifestyles that research had shown to exist. And marketers wonder why their messages aren't resonating with different groups.

It's Okay That Your Customers Are Different Than You

The one-way mirror of our research session was more than a device for observing consumers in an investigative setting. It was a wall that divided the "haves" from the "have-nots." On one side we have the customers telling us in their own words how they move through this world, and on the other side of the glass are marketing and advertising professionals refusing to take full advantage of the powerful insights and truths being shared with us.

"That can't be true" is the rationale for not listening, not connecting, and not understanding. We make the mistake of telling customers what we feel they need to hear (let's encourage them to meet our standard) instead of embracing the opportunity to get to know them and serving them where they are.

Times are changing, and so is the racial makeup of America. Marketers cannot afford to lag behind in learning how to build relationships with the growing multicultural segments, nor can marketers continue to attempt to force everyone to fit one standardized description. There is always going to be one big brand message, but inside that message should to be a multitude of smaller conversations that help to build and shape how people interact with a company or brand.

Learning to take part in all these conversations is the challenge facing marketers. Success comes from embracing the differences, and showing that companies understand and respect the individuality of the segments.

Is It "Black" or "African American"?

At the end of my presentations before groups, the number one question most often (privately) asked by White audience members is: "How do African Americans want to be addressed—Black or African American?"

It's a fair question, but the best answer I can offer requires a little back-story. The back-story is essential, because racial labels do make a difference, and getting them right, at the right time and, in the right context, means understanding and paying attention to societal shifts and trends.

I was born and raised in Chicago, but also lived with my family in the South during some of the most critical years of the Civil Rights movement, when I was aged 7 to 11. In grade school, I recall a heated squabble during recess between two boys in my fifth grade class. Although there were no punches thrown and I heard no cursing, things got loud and a crowd began to form. Finally, one of the teachers intervened. "He called me Black!" the accuser yelled when the teacher questioned them. Sympathetic oohs and ahs emerged from the sidelines. Back then, dubbing a person of African descent "Black," especially in the South, was roughly as offensive to Black people as Don Imus's infamous and slanderous comments about Rutgers University's women's basketball team in 2007.

There has been an evolution in the racial labels applied to African Americans over the years, one that has frequently proceeded simultaneously along multiple tracks. We were Negroes in the North, and colored in the South for the longest time. Then, in the 1960s, James Brown told us to stand up and proclaim our Blackness through a powerful, unforgettable personal anthem for Black people: "Say it Loud, I'm Black and I'm Proud!" In 1988, another phase of the evolution took place: the term African American became popular when Rev. Jesse Jackson held a news conference to encourage America to use it when referring to Blacks. However, since then, several societal shifts have caused a resurgence of the use of Black.

For one thing, the 2000 Census was the first to encourage people to self-select their race. This fueled more conscious discussions about where people fit in and how they preferred to be addressed.

In addition, the hip hop culture's mandate to "keep it real" helped reintroduce "Black" as a positive expression of intimacy and familiarity, which contrasted strongly with the negative baggage the phrase carried before and during the Civil Rights movement. We also saw an increase in the term's use among both African and Caribbean immigrants who preferred Black as a term reflecting acceptance as a thread within America's cultural fabric.

In 2008, when the question was posed to 3,400 African Americans for a "Black America Today" study, the two prevailing terms finished in almost a dead heat: 44 percent said they preferred Black, and 43 percent preferred African American. Only 11 percent didn't care.

Current trends indicate a slight preference for Black, in part because an increase in African and Caribbean immigrants. The current best answer to the question is that African American and Black are, at present, used interchangeably within the community these terms describe. I will be doing the same throughout this book.

Notes

1. Beth Snyder Bulik, "Marketers Still Don't Get How to Do Multicultural Marketing," *Advertising Age*, AdAge.com, February 25, 2008.

CHAPTER 1

The Profitable "Invisible Middle"[1]

Imagine making an estimated $150 million dollars from your stage plays with an estimated audience of 35,000 per week for the 300 shows per year that you produce, while most of America has no idea who you are.

It's not hard to imagine if you are Tyler Perry. Ranked by *Forbes* in 2011 as the sixth-highest-paid man in Hollywood and with a string of solid hit movies and two very popular TV sitcoms, Perry is realizing crossover success today. But even before this, success wasn't new for Perry. It is estimated that between 1990 and 2005, Perry's plays generated a gross income of about $150 million.

The people in beauty salons, barbershops, blue-collar workers and your lower-income people—those are the people that have been there for me since the beginning.   —Tyler Perry

By the Numbers

2010 Black Population: Hiding in Plain Sight

Black & Mixed	42 million or 13.6% of the U.S. population
Black Only	38.9 million or 12.6% of the U.S. population
24	The number of states in which Blacks are the largest minority group. Latinos are the largest minority group in 20 states

Source: U.S. Census Bureau

An accountant might think that to achieve his level of success, Perry has tapped into a huge mass market with his plays, movies and TV shows, but he hasn't. The secret to Perry's success lies in his ability to engage the segment of the market called "The Invisible Middle"™— Black Americans.

Black America tends to be viewed in extremes today, both by society at large and by marketers: there are the high-profile celebrities, entertainers, and sports figures on one side, and the impoverished, crime ridden, and down and out on the other. This flawed perception results in the rest of us—The Invisible Middle—being ignored or marginalized, according to the late Herb Kemp. He was the co-author of our African-American cultural marketing book, *What's Black About It?* and also coined the phrase "The Invisible Middle."

More than one homogenous group, the Invisible Middles are segmented by class, socio-economics, mindset, and a number of sub-segments that fly way under the average marketer's radar: Black LGBTs, Black biracials, Men, Women, Black Boomers, and Black Immigrants. Each will be discussed in future chapters.

How Perry Attracted the Invisible Middle

No stranger to his own audience segment, Perry faced his share of adversity at the extreme end of its spectrum, having endured a painful childhood and, for a time, homelessness. Leaning on his own experiences and knowledge, Perry was able to tap into a group that many marketers are either unable to see or refuse to acknowledge: working-class Blacks living satisfied, insular, lifestyles. This segment is more likely to be underexposed both socially and culturally than other groups, as they prefer to live, worship, and play exclusively in the Black community.

They're invisible because most people don't recognize them or hear from them. Few are asking their opinions or consider them a viable marketing target, but Perry's box office numbers and Nielsen ratings reflect their power. Perry's success originated from his "Chitlin Circuit" stage productions mentioned earlier. These plays followed a consistent formula: loud, slapstick productions that provided an additional—and often new—entertainment option for many working-class Blacks.

Although other Blacks often criticize Perry for his current and successful sit-coms, *House of Payne* and *Meet the Browns*, these programs have continued to hold top rankings for years as the cable TV shows most watched by Black audiences. Perry's audiences typically describe the shows as "funny" and "real," and often associate the characters with someone they know personally. They also strongly identify with hardship issues that Perry serves up such as drugs and addiction that often plague the Black community.

They don't see Perry's exploration of these issues as stereotypical or exploitative; instead their affinity with these shows is an appreciation for the positive resolution at the end of each episode. And it doesn't hurt that the shows carry the unspoken FUBU stamp: "For Us By Us."

Perry provides elements of truth, realism, and authenticity, and transforms them into entertainment escapism for a segment of the population that represents not only the unknown, but also the untouchables. Kemp may have named Perry's target audience the Invisible Middles, but Perry has recognized and used their available untapped buying power to become a visible Hollywood success story—for those willing to see.

Notes

1. A version of this chapter first appeared in *Advertising Age*, AdAge.com/bigtent.

CHAPTER 2

Why Marketers Say "No"— The Dynamics of Black Consumer Marketing

Everyday there are countless stories from within the African-American community and from the Black perspective that will never be given their fair weight of importance or be shared with the rest of the world. Even with the expansion of media through cable and the Internet, it seems as if we are still underserved when it comes to stories and issues that reflect and affect us.

—David A. Wilson, founder and former managing editor, *theGrio.com*

Being invisible doesn't mean being powerless. Tyler Perry's success only places a face on what the numbers have been showing for years.

The Selig Center for Economic Growth reports that the spending power of Black Americans was $957 billion in 2010.[1] Despite America's economic conditions, Black spending power continues to rise. Importantly, after tracking Black consumer buying power and spending on a wide range of products and services, *Target Market News'* 2010 annual report, "The Buying Power of Black America," highlights product categories where "Black households over-indexed, or outspent White households" for more than 15 consecutive years.[2]

Those categories include personal care products and services, men's and boys' footwear, telephone products and services, internet services, and home repair equipment and services.

Additionally, the Consumer Expenditure Survey conducted by the Department of Commerce reported that "the so-called over indexing by Black consumers in the food and apparel categories has been true for the past three decades that the survey has been taken."

Thus, Black Americans continue to place priority on buying food, beauty, fashion, entertainment and being the first to own the latest and greatest technological gadgets. Even so the marketers' response is to avoid the opportunity to increase their cultural intelligence about Black America and they have declined to invest appropriately in this market segment.

Today, many typical mass marketing models uphold and promote mainstream standards and insights with the expectations that everyone else will follow along. The thought that mainstream connectors will appeal to the majority is problematic. The question is not whether this is right or wrong *per se,* the question that needs to be asked is, "Why do marketers continue to say 'no' to understanding and speaking to Black consumers?"

Given not only the growth, but also the complexity of various ethnic (and other) segments, now more than ever, it is important for marketers to develop a new model that explores ethnicity and culture and the endless possibilities of connecting new segments with their brands. Then why haven't they done so?

There is no one set answer, but here are several reasons why marketers say no.

1. Language Has Become the Cultural Identifier

"They speak English don't they?" is the rhetorical question asked, and one rationale for not specifically connecting with Black America. As a result of the dynamic growth among Latinos and other ethnic segments that speak English as well as other languages, many marketers—unconsciously or not—see language as the cultural identifier, rather than attitudes and behavior. In their recent book, *Marketing to the New Majority* (Palgrave Macmillan, 2011), market research experts David Burgos and Ola Mobolade, validated the realities of targeted communications through their work at Millward Brown.

They took a stand and wrote this in support of targeted efforts:

"Based on our primary research for Millward Brown and our many experts in the field, we can affirm that, in general, targeted communication does a better job than non-targeted or mainstream advertising when trying to reach ethnic consumers. . . ."

"A common misconception about the African-American segment is that because Blacks speak English, and consume mainstream media, there is no need to develop any targeted communications to reach out to them. Yes, it is true that Black consumers are exposed to mainstream communication, but when it comes to an advertisement's effectiveness, our data clearly suggest that well-crafted targeted initiatives do a better job than mainstream campaigns."[3]

The primary focus on language versus gleaning insights from attitudes and behavior has caused many marketers to miss the opportunity to gain a deeper understanding of Black Americans, which results in failing to better connect with Black Americans in a meaningful way.

2. Looking Beyond Ethnicity, Culture and Race: The Hazards of "Progressive" Thinking

They [marketers] need to step out of the comfort of their own culture to be effective in another. . . .[4]

Marketers like to think they are "enlightened" or "progressive" in their thinking concerning race, that they've grown beyond seeing people based on their color or race, that they simply see people.

While this idea is noble in thought and intent, it is dangerous in its application. In trying to see everyone as the same, marketers fail to see people for who they really are. Being "enlightened" or "progressive" means accepting people for who they are, not trying to make them all the same.

I love Mary Lou Quinlan's book, *What She's Not Telling You.* Quinlan and co-authors, Jen Dexler and Tracy Chapman, reveal eye-opening half and whole truths that women often tell marketers. It's an interesting premise for understanding women's (human) behavior. The authors challenge the current marketing model and uncover why it has not been successful connecting with women in a relevant way. (So many lessons here for multicultural marketers!) And, being a researcher, I was drawn to their critique of how some marketers mishandle the focus group process—particularly their discussion about how ineffective screening and listening can result in totally misunderstanding women. The book also includes a number of interesting case studies and the authors' point-of-view about ad campaigns that worked, those that didn't, and insightful "things to think about in a different way" sidebars. But early on, I disagree with Quinlan, she writes:

> "For whatever reason, marketers often like to focus more on women's differences, preferring fine-toothed segmentation and consumer algorithms that split hairs instead of commonalities that can actually be marketed to. We think they're missing the forest for the trees."[5]

Unfortunately, Quinlan, like many marketers, is missing the trees. The next big thing is a lot of little things. It's the trees, not the forest.

In her poignantly written post on *Ad Age*'s multicultural blog, *The Big Tent*, Rochelle Newman-Carrasco criticizes the current mainstream marketing model under the headline: "What Gladwell's *Outliers* Can Teach You About Marketing."[6] Under the last of Carrasco's four-point "how to" message, she writes:

> "We think it is progressive to 'see beyond' race and culture vs. to be at ease with acknowledging their existence. . . . there are those who criticize the use of culture, ethnicity, race or other related variables as being inappropriate, racist, insensitive or segregationist, to name a few perceived drawbacks. In-school and at-work politeness techniques, sometimes taught in the guise of diversity training, encourage us to think of people 'as one' vs. 'as many.' Along these lines, there are those

who assert that there is no race, just the human race. It's simply not the case. Nor, in my opinion, is it forward thinking to believe it is. What is important for our collective futures is to acknowledge race, ethnicity and culture and to stop judging it."

Carrasco's point encapsulates and underscores the overarching message of this book. Blackness, culture, history, ethnicity, and identity matter.

The cliché, "The Browning of America" is real. Given America's population shifts, now is the time to better understand the different population segments so that marketers can plan effectively. Instead, many are prone to look exclusively for commonalities and often justify their thinking with rationales discussed in this section including "I don't see race when I see a Black person," which have always bothered me.

The problem with discussing race and the Black community is Black history. There's a lot of pain and shame associated with Black history for many Blacks and Whites. (*See* History, Culture, and Differences Matter, *page 29*). Many in society, who fail to understand the impact of the pain and shame of slavery on Black Americans and this country, are quick to denounce these teachings as racist. Thus, society's modern day sentiment is to avoid discussions about the history of slavery, post slavery, and discrimination. Unfortunately, when we follow this mindset we all lose.

Black Americans lose because there is a tremendous amount of valuable history tied to their self-esteem and identity.

Society and marketers lose because they fail to understand that Black history—the good, the bad and the really ugly—are important to the conundrum surrounding Black culture: Black America's overwhelming desire to be respected and treated equally in the U.S. and globally.

Additionally, American culture suggests that successful persons of color, who are elevated to high level positions, abandon their culture and heritage and, particularly for African Americans, their "Blackness."

Unfortunately, this practice fails to move the agenda forward, and makes it difficult for those persons to speak to the needs of any particular group.

I get the "We are the human race" and "people are people" mantras, but they are not enough to unearth the nuggets of emotions that are critical for brand connectivity within the new mainstream. I also understand how uncomfortable it is to talk about race. People are afraid of being targeted as being divisive if they introduce race as a topic. I assure you, it's divisive not to talk about race. A recent post on CNN.com reveals the differences in how Black and White parents deal with race with their young children:

> People are afraid of being targeted as being divisive if they introduce race as a topic. I assure you, it's divisive to *not* talk about race.

A 2007 study in the *Journal of Marriage and Family* found that 75 percent of White families with kindergartners never, or almost never, talk about race. For Black parents the number is reversed with 75 percent addressing race with their children.

One of the major findings in a CNN pilot study on children's attitudes about race is that White children have an overwhelming bias toward White, and that Black children also have a bias toward White but not nearly as strong as the bias shown by the White children.

CNN also reported that Po Bronson, author of *NurtureShock* (Twelve, 2011) and an award-winning writer on parenting issues says White parents "want to give their kids this sort of post-racial future when they're very young and they're under the wrong conclusion that their kids are colorblind. . . . It's in the absence of messages of tolerance that they will naturally . . . develop these skin preferences."

Many African-American parents CNN spoke to during the study say they begin discussing race at a very early age because they feel they have to prepare their children for a society where their skin color will create obstacles for them.

The changing American population provides the opportunity for learning about the differences as well as for embracing the similarities and not labeling or limiting people's possibilities just because they are different.

"Different is not deficient." [7]

We will need some form of ethnic marketing and its insights as long as society excludes, judges, misunderstands, and discriminates against groups of people based on their inalienable characteristics.

> *People may mean well, but when they say they don't see race, it's another way of saying they don't want to see race. People should be proud to see African American, Asian and Latino . . .*
> —Jonathan Jackson, Civil Rights and Human Activist;
> professor, City Colleges of Chicago

3. The Generational Divide = Post-Racial Society
The Boomerang Effect and the Generational Divide:
The Youth Generation Isn't as mainstream as it appears

"The Millennials will save us, the Millennials will save us!"

I hope so; I sincerely hope so.

Many marketers believe that growing up in a multicultural world, Millennials will usher in the age of "post-racial" America, that this group will eliminate the need to speak to different segments and groups. And to be honest, it is easy to see how they have arrived at this conclusion.

Millennials and younger GenXers born after the Civil Rights struggles—share a different mindset from those born before or during the Civil Rights Era (although many would argue that the Civil Rights Era is not over yet). Parents and children have been seeing the world differently forever. So, it should not be a shock that the generational divide in the African-American community is primarily based on pre- and post-civil rights mindsets—those born before and during the Civil Rights Era (Silent Generation and Boomers) and those born after (Echo Boomers, Millennials, and younger GenXers).

The Post-Racial Mindset

"Why do we have to keep talking about race? Why can't we just move past it?"

Tim and Cathy are "new mainstreamers"—as they see it. They are not their parents, and they proudly own that. Like their parents, they see themselves as good, hard-working people who choose suburban life primarily for their children. Their kids attend one of the best public schools in their community. Compared with the composition of the student population when they were attending grammar and high school, the student body at their children's school is 80 percent White. Tim and Cathy consider it "very" diverse.

Although they don't have any close relationships with people of color, they consider themselves to be more open-minded than their parents. Recently Tim and Cathy hosted a sleepover for their daughter. They were delighted and welcoming to the Black child that was part of the group of nine 10-year-old girls. They believe "post-racial America" is a bit wobbly, but is finally here, yet (unknowingly like their parents) are uncomfortable discussing race.

"We have a Black president. We voted for him. Many of our friends voted for him. We recently had a little Black girl spend the night in our house—that would have never happened when I was growing up—and my son's math tutor is East Indian. The value of accepting others is reflected in our children. They are teaching us and they are the future. We need to stop talking about race. Post Racial America is here. People are people for God's sake. We're all from the human race. Let's get past this and move on."

Making statements like this or asking why we can't move past the "race" thing only highlights how far we have to go. The "post-racial America" view skips a very important step of recognizing the culture and differences between Blacks and other minorities. Tim and Cathy are more open and accepting, but they still only see the world through their eyes. How accepting and open are they really?

Millennials celebrate and embrace multiculturalism, and are generally optimistic. They're fiends for technology and for many, their social identity is intertwined with technology. And due to the overzealous nature of many parents today who don't want their children to feel the roller coaster emotions of life's disappointments, Millennials tend to take entitlement to a whole new level, as many believe all they have to do to get anything is just to show up.

The Boomerang Effect

Black youth follow this same mindset and behavior except they tend to be even more complex given the "boomerang effect"—the "history" that many Millennials avoid early on, they later come to embrace.

To be clear, we as a country are moving towards a truly inclusive multicultural society. And our youth are the key. We are seeing more progress each day, but we cannot ignore that we are still a distance from where we all want to be. Thus, it is paramount to the success of any marketing effort that this generational divide be recognized and addressed.

There are solid and well documented examples of the differences between the groups.

According to The Radio-One Black America Study, many teens and Millennials shun Boomers' "oppressive" talk. In his book *The Hip Hop Generation* (Basic Civitas Books, 2003), Bakari Kitwana reveals that some younger Blacks describe Boomers and other older African Americans as "the enemy from within." Kitwana explains that the younger generation's criticism of the older generation's need to embrace pre-civil rights history and openly express their feelings about race and racism "holds the Black community back." However, in focus group research, Black Millennials, like their Black Boomer predecessors, scrutinize ads for positive images, yet are also more likely than Boomers to challenge the racial composition of ads that feature an all Black cast.

Marketers take insights like this as justification for slashing or eliminating Black consumer marketing budgets. In August 2010, Burger King consolidated its advertising by shifting its assignments from African-American and Latino agencies to a mainstream agency, "citing the X and Y generations" and their beliefs in the "melting pot."

Houston, we have a problem. While we are moving towards a post-racial society, we don't live in a post-racial society today. Not yet.

Consider Carl's story:

> "I am a Black man that owns a communications firm. This is not a Black business . . . I am a mainstream marketer."

This is the message that Carl wanted me to come away with after visiting his southern-based ad agency in 2004—the year it opened. Carl was psyched. He also exercised a bit of harmless boasting and bravado as if to let me know that he was going to teach Boomer advertising executives a lesson or two—especially Black advertising executives—given that none led large mainstream agencies.

"Uh-huh," I thought to myself, "good luck with that."

Seven years later while reviewing his updated website, I looked admirably at all the Black work displayed under the "Clients" and "Case Studies" tabs, and couldn't help but reflect on our conversation years earlier.

Carl's experiences mirror mine from the late 1980s. Like me, when Carl showed up to pitch general market companies for mainstream business, he too was only given "Black" assignments. He's proud of the work he has done, and welcomes the opportunity to practice his craft, yet he is also disappointed that he hasn't been able to steer his agency into the mainstream space. He sees himself as an "equal" to his mainstream counterparts: Ivy League education, general market ad agency and consumer package goods company experience, smart, well-spoken and great ideas, but is disappointed nonetheless.

And if this isn't enough, he reads in the trades and industry blogs that marketing experts and some colleagues question why businesses like his would deliberately "pigeon-hole" themselves in the Black space.

Although Carl's agency is poised to use its intellect and strategies to connect brands with the new mainstream, he has embraced Black/

Urban consumer marketing and is motivated to take the category to higher level.

The boomerang effect is also an indication of how many Black Millennials are realizing that Black is beautiful . . . again.

For many, particularly those that have had a long-term urban experience, being Black and being successful does not mean having to emulate mainstream and society's definition of success. Instead they are recognizing that with a shift to a more global, more diverse society, being Black has value. For example:

- Black bloggers created the annual Blogging While Black (now, Blogging While Brown) conference "to give Bloggers of Color an opportunity to meet each other, discuss current issues affecting Bloggers of Color, and learn about the latest technology that will assist them with publishing their work."

- Mocha Moms was launched in 1997 to recognize African-American families who were participating in the trend of women of color leaving full-time employment to raise their children. It has since exploded with several chapters across the country.

- David A. Wilson directed and wrote the critically acclaimed MSNBC documentary, *Meeting David Wilson*, a film that chronicled his personal journey to find answers to today's racial disparities in America. As founder and former managing editor of theGrio.com, Wilson partnered with NBC to create this first video-centric news community site. TheGrio.com is devoted to providing African Americans with stories and perspectives that appeal to them but are under-represented in existing national news outlets.

- After running into roadblock after roadblock, Neil Nelson and business partner, Iziah Reid, decided to shuck their dream of building digital platforms for mainstream companies and build their own for urban consumers. Today, they own DimeWars.com (Daily Insights, Music & Entertainment) a leading urban-entertainment, online news property. Launched in the summer of 2008, dimewars.com provides "fresh relevant content including haps in hip-hop music, urban culture, sports highlights, politics, cool gadgets, fashion and, occasionally a little finance, and is one of the top five leaders of the urban online news daily 'must-visits' for entertainment industry professionals and fans alike."

Additionally, although Millennials are the most sheltered generation by their Boomer parents, Black Millennials are not immune to the messages and experiences that Black life presents. For example, Bossip.com, rollingout.com, and dimewars.com, popular online gossip and entertainment sites targeted to the young Black audience not only post information about noted celebrities, they also include current news stories and videos about politics, people, and groups who are considered controversial to this segment such as Sarah Palin, Glenn Beck, and the Tea Party. (*See* Blacks in Cyberspace, *page 173*)

Then, there is Qasim Basir (pronounced Ka-*sim* Ba-*seer*), writer and director of the successful national and international film, *Mooz-Lum*. It highlights the struggles of Tariq Mahdi, a Black Muslim and first-year college student pulled between his strict Muslim upbringing by his father and the normal social life he's never had. The movie stars popular actors Danny Glover, Nia Long, Dorian Missick, and Evan Ross as Tariq. I spoke with Basir who, at the time of our interview, was 29 and is also Black and Muslim. He shared his personal agenda for creating this movie:

"In the last decade there have been constant negative portrayals of Muslims in the news and media and it's been troubling me for a long time. I wrote the script in an attempt to explain the human side of Muslim people."

Basir talked openly about his own post 9/11 experiences that, interestingly, in no way, resemble the Millennial Kumbaya theories about race in America:

"After 9/11 a lot changed for Muslim people in America. It became even more difficult to travel. Post 9/11, as you can imagine, has been the worst.

"When I tell people I am Muslim, they treat you differently. On one flight, I was in the middle seat between these two White guys. We were laughing and talking—having a great conversation. One asked what I did and I told him: 'I'm a film writer and director.' They thought that was cool until we formally introduced ourselves. They asked if I was a Muslim. 'Yes I am.' I said proudly, and the conversation was over, just like that."

Basir leaves us with one final comment: "The ideals of America are great. I love this country!" says Basir with all sincerity. "It's the only place I could have succeeded in doing what I do. But I totally disagree with how America responds to the Muslim community. I'm hoping that (with this film), people will relate to us more, instead of portraying us as demons."

The 2009 IMAGES USA Millennials Study reveals that Black Millennials are more likely to take a stand on political issues, and are galvanized around their identity to show a strong sense of purpose. During the Jena Six trials, more than 50,000 mostly young people descended on the small town of Jena, Louisiana in support of six Black teenagers convicted in the beating of Justin Barker, a White student at Jena High School, on December 4, 2006.

There comes a point when how they believe the world "should be" comes into conflict with how the world "is." Sadly, Black Millennials discover the old folks knew what they were talking about.

By understanding the contrast between the hopes and dreams for a multicultural society and the reality of our society today, marketers can better craft messages that reflect a deeper understanding of the audience they are trying to reach, bridging the generational divide for greater success.

4. Black America Can't Afford to Buy

Black folks aren't poor, they're just broke.
—George Fraser, motivational speaker, networking guru; author of
Click: Ten Truths for Building Extraordinary Relationships

There's a value in understanding how the mindset that Fraser references affects spending in the African-American community. Since the economic downturn, two dichotomous conversations are ongoing in the Black community:

America's response to the recession: curb spending; focus on making ends meet. The climate for many Blacks is worse and therefore recession translates to a depression for Black America.

At the same time, for many African-Americans, the recession/depression climate is not necessarily new, and many quickly adapt.

The new normal for middle-class America has been the old normal or standard for many in the Black community. Lay-away, for example, is a new idea for many retailers to lure mainstream shoppers to their stores. But for African Americans, lay-away has been the norm, a way of life. Black folks would lay-away a car, or house if they could.

Given Black America's economic history and experiences, the idea of what is poor and how it impacts the community has to be looked at differently.

The Institute on Assets and Social Policy (IASP) at Brandeis University reported that the racial wealth gap between White and African-American families increased more than four times between 1984 and 2007, and middle-income White households now own far more wealth than high-income African Americans. The average middle-income White household had accumulated $74,000 in wealth, an increase of $55,000 over the 23-year period, while the average high-income African-American family owned $18,000, a drop of $7,000.

That resulted in a wealth gap of $56,000 for an African-American family that earned more than $50,000 in 1984 compared with a White family earning about $30,000 that same year.[8]

The article goes on to outline the barriers to wealth among African Americans and the need for new policies to help reduce and ultimately eliminate the wealth gap. (*See* The MOSES Movement, *page 25*)

The National Urban League's annual *State of Black America Report* typically paints a truthful, but often dismal, picture about the current situation and outlook of Black America. While this information is not inaccurate, the Urban League and many service organizations typically rely on some of the harsh realities of Black America to secure grants and funding for social service and economic development programs that are sorely needed and appreciated by Black communities across the nation.

I am not, by any means, suggesting that abject poverty does not exist in the Black community. As I write this, the unemployment rate for Blacks surged to 16.7 percent in August 2011, its highest rate since 1984, according to the Labor Department. Nor am I implying that the social service reports and studies mentioned earlier are not welcomed or valued. They are. However, marketers who read these studies often use them to drive the last nail in the Black community's coffin and use "poor economics in the Black community" as a reason not to consider them as a viable market segment. For many Black Americans, the standards and definition of what poor is, and what poor means vary based on their mindset, perceptions, and their resourcefulness.

The underground economy or black market is often linked with illegal activities such as drugs and gambling. In ethnic communities, the underground economy includes trades, goods and services that are not part of the official economy (i.e., home-based hairstylists, home caretakers, babysitters, handymen, "alley mechanics," the candy lady, etc.). These "jobs" provide an important, albeit under the radar, contribution to Black spending power.

Lower-income households: The new frontier

Nielsen data show the lowest income population segment growing the fastest as much as 17.8 percent in some scenarios with affluent and wealthy segments declining (9.2% and 5.5% respectively.)[9]

In fact, Symphony IRI released a ground-breaking study, *The 2010 Lower-Income Multicultural Shopper Study*. It explores shopping attitudes and behaviors of African-American, Latino, and Asian lower-income shoppers and concludes that the lower-income shopper segment is an important growth segment that will drive $115 billion in incremental spending in food and non-food categories within the next 10 years. During a September 2010 webinar, Symphony IRI study architects Sean Seitsinger and Brent Baarda presented some fascinating highlights from the study. Here are a few lower-income shopper myth busters that they shared:

Myth #1	Lower-income shoppers spend less than higher-income households and therefore, represent a smaller economic opportunity.
Truth	In the last 3 years, lower-income households have outpaced spending in middle- and higher-income households.
Myth #2	Lower-income households share the same tendencies.
Truth	There are huge variations and spending levels across a variety of categories, and in some cases lower-income households are more motivated to find health and wellness brands than high-income shoppers.
Myth #3	Lower-income shoppers are less profitable because they only buy value brands.
Truth	Lower-income shoppers are interested in good value. Not just "cheap" but value is important. They want different ways to access value (i.e., national brands in smaller packages).

In fact, African-American lower-income consumers make the most retail shopping trips per year with 177 trips, seniors make 169, and Hispanics make 168. Lower-income households with children spend the most per trip at $39.65, followed by younger households at $37.58.

Although lower- and higher-income shoppers both report careful trip planning, more than half of ethnic shoppers routinely make unplanned purchases while in the store.

Sean Seitsinger is also opposed to using a one-size strategy for reaching low-income shoppers, and added this comment during the webinar:

". . . one of the great challenges of accessing those growth dollars is understanding the diversity of needs and opportunities that are going to create that additional $115 billion. Going to market with a one-size-fits-all approach to serve low-income consumers really isn't going to be successful. It's going to be about understanding how diverse this group is and how different and unique some of their needs are so that you can pick the places where you want to play with low-income and multicultural segments."

By the Numbers

2010 Black Population: Hiding in Plain Sight

177	The number of retail shopping trips made per year by African-American shoppers
$115 billion	Potential additional dollars per year associated with understanding ethnic shoppers

Source: The Multicultural Economy, *Selig Center for Economic Growth, 2011*

||||||||||||||||||||||||||||||||||||||

STORIES

"It's not how much money you have, it's what you do with it."

Dana (pronounced *Donna*) Thompson is a no-nonsense single mother of five daughters. Four of the girls are single parents too. They live independently from their mother, and are working at being good moms. Dana's youngest, a 17-year-old and the last at home, is doing well in school. She holds down a 3.5 GPA and aspires to be a lawyer.

Dana has supported her family over the years by providing home and office cleaning services. She's the sole employee, and a hard worker. Dana would be assigned to the lower-income households according to society's standards, and yet 12 years ago she purchased a house and is doing well with the payments and upkeep. In fact, since the purchase, she has invested in major maintenance items such as windows and a roof, a wrought iron fence, and is saving for a new front porch. And she's always, always decorating—painting, wallpapering, updating the bathroom with towels, rugs and accessories, and is forever changing the furniture around. She even created a "learning room" for her grandchildren. The walls are lovingly crammed with posters of alphabets, phonics, mathematics, and Black History learning aids. The bookcases and shelves are filled with books, school supplies and educational games.

Dana lives, works, socializes and shops (for food and clothing) in the Black community and occasionally ventures out of the community to clothes shop and dine at casual dining restaurants like Applebee's. She enjoys spending time with her daughters, grandchildren and girlfriends. She also likes Facebook and playing online video games.

Food is a really big deal in Dana's household. It's the nucleus that brings people that she loves together especially given that she doesn't eat out very often.

Born on the Fourth of July, Dana celebrates her birthday with a small gathering at her home every year. For a recent milestone birthday, Dana had a big celebration, and the food was in abundance. She proudly pulled back the aluminum foil–covered dishes to allow me a sneak peak at the bounty: jumbo shrimp, thick meaty ribs, chicken, fish, a variety of side dishes and desserts. For Dana, and many African Americans, large quantities of food served during birthdays, Sunday dinners, and holiday meals is common and is perceived as a badge of sorts, even when food contributions are from others.

When food shopping, Dana purchases both national and store brands. Her decision to purchase a particular brand is based on value. Taste, the quality of ingredients, consistency (product performance over time) and brand reputation is the value she expects from national brands, and the reason why Dana chooses particular national brands over store brands. Price for these brands is not a factor. On the other hand, the ingredients, product and packaging, and price are the barometer for selecting store brands over some national brands.

Dana relies on traditional media. She listens to a lot of radio and spends a fair amount of time watching television to relax. She pays attention to advertising, learns about new products and services from radio, television and word of mouth, and like many Black Americans, is particularly drawn to ads and messages that feature Black Americans.

Dana is a good person, wants to do right by her family and community and is an influencer and "she-ro" among her family and peers.

She tends to live day-to-day and was doing so as a way of life long before the economic downturn. At the same time, she understands value and the importance of saving—based on her needs—not by society's standards. Given this different point of view, Dana and others like her are a forgotten and underserved segment.

The opportunity is to connect with Dana and understand her story. Dana and many like her are prime candidates for food, entertainment, fashions (for herself, daughters, and grandchildren), beauty, home improvements, automobiles, mobile phones, and financial services.

———

Black and affluent

In spite of the economic downturn, Black buying power continues to increase. "The increase in Black buying power stems from more Blacks who are better educated and who are earning higher incomes," says Dr. Jeffery Humphreys, director of the Selig Center for Economic Growth, developers and gatekeepers of consumer buying power statistics for various U.S. populations.

About one third of Black Americans rank as "affluent" (annual income of $75,000 or more), with an average annual household income of $122,000. The number of African-American households earning $75,000 or more has grown by 63.9 percent in the last decade, a rate greater than that of the overall population.[10] Although Black affluents represent only 17 percent of all African-American households, they wield 45 percent of the total purchasing power in the African-American market.

Leonard Burnett Jr. (co-CEO and group publisher of Uptown Media Group and Vibe Lifestyle Network) and Andrea Hoffman (CEO of consultancy Diversity Affluence) challenge luxury marketers to take a closer look at affluent African Americans in their book, *Black Is the New Green: Marketing to Affluent African Americans* (Palgrave Macmillan, 2010). Citing cultural attitudinal and behavioral insights surrounding this segment, Hoffman and Burnett make the case that luxury marketers are missing out on a lucrative market. In an article for reachingblackconsumers.com, Hoffman and Deborah McNally, marketing consultant with Diversity Affluence write about these insights:

They want the best. Affluent African-American consumers are comfortable with treating themselves to the very best.

Opportunity segments include luxury travel, fine dining, luxury automobiles, personal services, luxury home items, designer apparel, and high-end liquors and wines.

They seek exclusivity. Affluent African-American consumers are driven by the desire to purchase (and learn about or have access to) something not everyone can afford.

They are aspirational. Affluent African-American consumers are focused on "trading up" to more luxurious brands and experiences.

They conduct research. Although some purchases are impulsive, for the most part affluent African-American consumers conduct extensive research on an item prior to purchase (e.g., internet surfing).

They seek value as often as possible. Luxury items mean value in that they last longer and the brand name stands behind its product. This consumer's attitude is: It's not how much you make but how much you keep.

Hoffman and McNally add:

"Affluent African Americans differ from the urban/Hip-Hop crowd in several significant ways. Tending to be highly educated urbanites who own their own homes, affluent African Americans spend their disposable income on very different purchases from the urban or Hip-Hop crowds, and they are less-conspicuous consumers. While African-American athletes, entertainers and actors stand out as conspicuous consumers of luxury goods, a larger segment of affluents are conservative entrepreneurs, executives and professionals, and they are just as powerful and influential but under the radar."

Brands that recognize this can capture a share of this group's purchasing power, and it can be done via affordable grassroots, niche and target marketing.[12]

STORIES

Let My People Grow: The MOSES Movement

As mentioned earlier, Black Americans spent $957 billion in 2010. But how much did they save? Unfortunately not much. According to the Prudential Insurance Study, *The African American Financial Experience* (April 2011), 60% of African Americans surveyed have less than $50,000 in company retirement plans, and only 23% have more than $100,000.

Additionally, according to a report by the FDIC (December 2009), just over 25% of the U.S. population is unbanked (i.e., household with no checking or savings accounts) or underbanked (i.e., household checking or savings account exists, but alternate financial services provide for most household business transactions). African-American households represent the greatest share in both categories.

	Unbanked	Underbanked
African American	21.7%	31.6%
White	3.3	14.9
Hispanic	19.3	24.0
Asian	3.5	7.2

Source: FDIC, 2009

But George Fraser has a plan—a design to move African Americans from the bondage of financial ignorance and poverty to the promised land of economic security and success. Fraser is CEO of FraserNet, Inc., a company he founded 20 years ago with the vision to lead a global networking movement that brings together diverse human resources to increase opportunities for people of African descent. He is considered by many to be a new voice for African Americans and one of the foremost authorities on economic development, networking, and building effective relationships.

He had this to say about Black Americans' financial position and Black Boomers' responsibility to help:

Black Baby Boomers will be the first generation to raise another generation that will not do better than themselves, according to Fraser. This is the first generation with this distinction in 400 years. "We (Boomers) need our butts kicked and I will not be a part of this irresponsible legacy."

To address the issue head on, Fraser created The MOSES (Making Our Selves Economically Successful) Movement[SM], a comprehensive step-by-step program designed to educate and motivate African Americans to become financially literate, including being securely banked, invested and insured.

In collaboration with Cheryl D. Broussard, an award-winning author and one of America's leading experts on business and personal finance, and others who are some of the keenest Black financial minds in the country, The MOSES Movement is rooted in "10 Commitments for Financial Freedom," an inspirational and spiritual pledge by African Americans to upgrade their financial positioning through education, discipline, and more importantly by taking action.

The MOSES Movement has a three-pronged plan. EVERYONE can gain control through personal commitment, by learning to manage their savings and then their credit. The means to these objectives are conveniently available through online course materials on "Money Mastery" and webinars. The project launched in November 2011.

George Fraser made a personal choice against mighty odds that led to his success, personally and professionally. His MOSES Movement speaks to the need for the development of financial products that serve people where they are, and clears the way for many others to follow.

———

5. The Budget

Or little or no budget, I should say. In this economy, it isn't a question of fighting over a smaller *piece* of the budgetary pie; departments are fighting over a smaller budgetary pie!

No department is hit more often or harder than the marketing department. Even today, many companies struggle with recognizing marketing as a necessity, rather than an option.

Yet, as the budgets are getting tighter, companies are trying even harder to expand their reach, looking for more business and new opportunities. They're asking their marketers to do more with less, making it harder to justify taking a risk or trying something different. In response to this demand, most marketers tend to play it safe and go with the familiar hoping to carve out some measure of success, instead of marketing to a segment that they are not familiar with.

At the exact moment when marketers really need to be focusing a greater portion of their attention on the African-American market, they are reducing the dollars allocated to the Black consumer segment.

Budgetary constraints are not the only part of the decision to forego marketing to Black consumers, but are part of a decision-making process that can also include any or all of the aforementioned four reasons as part of the determining factors for saying, "no." However, the data don't lie. There is gold in marketing to Black consumers.

The African-American community makes up 13.6 percent of the population of the United States and is projected to reach 14 percent over the next 10 years. This equates to populations of 42 million and nearly 48 million for 2010 and 2020, respectively. The growth rate for African-Americans outpaces that of the total population by almost 30 percent and reflects not only an increase in people, but also their affluence and influence.[12]

By the Numbers

Black Ad Spending: A Drop in the Bucket

$1.9 billion	total Black advertising spending
$263.7 billion	total U.S. advertising spending

Source: State of the African-American Consumer, *The Nielsen Company, 2011*

New media outlets, innovative programming, and relevant content continue to emerge from existing Black media companies and Black entrepreneurs, receiving record use by Black audiences. However, of the $263.7 billion spent annually on U.S. advertising, total advertising spend in African-American media was only $1.9 billion in 2010, albeit a 3 percent increase over 2009.[13]

Spending power, population growth, affluence, and influence continue to be undervalued. Saying, "no" to marketing to Black consumers based on budget no longer makes dollars and cents . . . or sense.

Notes

1. Selig Center for Economic Growth, *The Multicultural Economy*, 2011.
2. Ken Smikle, "Over-indexing by Black Consumers Is Missed Learning Opportunity for Marketers," *Target Market News*, April 21, 2010.
3. David Burgos and Ola Mobolade, *Marketing to the New Majority* (New York: Palgrave Macmillan, 2011).
4. Felipe Korzenny, "Marketing Trends in a New Multicultural Society—All Marketing Is Cultural," felipekorzenny.blogspot.com, March 25, 2010.
5. Mary Lou Quinlan, Jen Drexler, and Tracy Chapman, *What She's Not Telling You* (Austin, Texas, Greenleaf Publishers, 2010), 18.
6. Rachel Newman-Carrasco, "What Gladwell's Outliers Can Teach You about Marketing," *Advertising Age*, AdAge.com/bigtent, March 2, 2009.
7. Jeremiah A. Wright, Jr., Pastor Emeritus, Trinity United Church of Christ, Chicago.
8. "New Study Says Wealth Gap between Blacks and Whites Has Quadrupled Since Mid 1980s," *Target Market News*, targetmarketnews.com, May 20, 2010.
9. "Nielsen: Ethnic and Low-income Consumers Driving Future Packaged Good Trends," *Target Market News*, targetmarketnews.com, May 15, 2009.
10. Nielsen and National Newspapers Association, "The State of the African-American Consumer," September 2011.
11. Andrea Hoffman and Deborah McNally, "Marketing to Affluent African Americans," www.reachingblackconsumers.com.
12. *Nielsen and National Newspapers Association, "The State,"* op. cit.
13. Ibid., and David Alexander, "Black Buying Power: Watch Where You Spend Your Money," *www.ourweekly.com*, August 18, 2011.

CHAPTER 3

Black America Today: It's STILL a Different World
History, Culture, and Differences Matter

It's often said, "history is written by the victor," but that doesn't mean that it is viewed the same by every ethnic group or shapes how that group perceives and interacts with the world.

Each group sees the world through a series of lenses or filters that are based on their history. This happens both on a group and personal level. The psychology of our current and past experiences can have an astounding effect on how we see ourselves, how we perceive the world, and how we perceive how the world sees us.

Consider the morbidly overweight man, who worked tirelessly to get his svelte physique yet who still sees "the fat guy" when he looks at himself in the mirror, or the "Silent Generation" who lived through the Great Depression who, in an attempt to avoid the feelings associated with situations of lack, become great savers or reckless spenders. Situations and events in our history shape our views and beliefs.

History, be it personal or communal, matters.

The African-American Filter

The African-American filter is a historical and cultural lens with distinguishing characteristics that explains why most African Americans are culturally different as citizens and consumers. However, in an attempt to be seen as "advanced" or "post racial," many marketers mistakenly choose to ignore differences among cultures, and instead try to view people through the same lens.

Failing to understand this historical filter and its impact on Black culture widens the existing chasm of misunderstanding and discord.

In 1994, the country was strained and racially divided during the O.J. Simpson trials. One event in time, two dramatically different views. Blacks viewing this through a lens created from years of negative interaction saw a justice system weighted against them, and therefore saw the trial as a test of the entire justice system—could it really be fair?

Whites viewing it through a lens created from years of mainly positive interaction with the justice system saw the trial as a test of guilt or innocence and nothing else. While they recognized that the system may not be perfect, they believed that it is fair and just most of the time.

Looking back, it is easy to see how these two views of the same point and time in history could produce dramatically different responses.

When Simpson was pronounced "not guilty" for the murders of his ex-wife Nicole Brown Simpson and her friend Ron Goldman, the split screen television images of Blacks cheering versus the look of shock, horror, and disbelief among Whites, were astonishing and very telling.

Without an adequate understanding of the two different views, it was hard for people on either side to understand the other. We should not be surprised.

Whites believed the Black community to be hardhearted and insensitive toward the victims and their families, which was far from the truth. Most Blacks sympathized and prayed for the Brown, Simpson, and Goldman families. For many Blacks, justice was on trial (not O.J.), and the system worked in their favor instead of against it.

Finally, for an instant in time, Blacks realized the promise of a system that looked beyond race and color. For a moment, respect on a national level, even for a moment, was in reach.

Fast forward to the Presidency of Barack Obama. The country is again divided, not only politically but racially as well. "The more things change, the more they stay the same." Although the country has elected its first African-American President, many in the Black community see and feel a familiar undertone to how the President of the United States of America is treated. And no one came to represent this trend more than Donald Trump.

The "birther" movement was an annoyance for me. I usually push past heavily hyped news stories like this. I can be happy, sad, or neutral in the moment, and move on, but then came Donald Trump. The Trump-led birther movement really got to me. Never in our history has a U.S. President had to publicly show proof of his citizenship.

Something about Trump's antics reminded me of my experiences as a young child living in the segregated South. During those pre- and early post-Civil Rights days while extremists used misinformation and half truths to vilify Blacks, America watched silently without acting until the rhetoric encouraged someone to commit some unthinkable or horrible act that resulted in the loss of life or injury, instead of addressing the message that led up to it.

For more than three years birthers attacked the citizenship of the President, dismissing his original birth certificate. It took a CNN investigation, a release of his long form birth certificate, and two key players at the White House Press Corps dinner—the President of the United States and Seth Meyers, the insightful, brave, quick-witted, head writer from *Saturday Night Live*—to denounce the lack of facts supporting the birther argument and put an end to Donald Trump's antics. Finally, Trump was exposed.

Trump's behavior not only disrespected Barack Obama and the office of the Presidency, but he opened up old wounds in the Black community.

Many Blacks perceive the birther message—along with the "take back our country" mantra of the Tea Party groups—as more than an attack on the President. It's also seen as an attempt to remind Blacks of their place.

Even so, there's a silver lining in this dark, dark cloud. Here are four lessons for which we can thank Donald Trump:

1. **Trump helped jump-start engaging conversations about racism in the U.S., helping America break her silence. Finally, we are talking about race—really talking.** Trump's words and actions ignited a fire. Sure the regular cast of characters, journalists, and celebrities were speaking out against Trump and racial practices in America, but through the digital realm, many others were taking part in the conversation. People from all aspects of society were tweeting, blogging, and expressing their thoughts on the issue. A dialogue was started. America was really talking about how we see and treat each other. Not only did this spur conversation, there was also action. Through social media, many demanded that Trump be dropped from the Indy 500—one of the "Whitest" sporting events in the United States. Trump pulled out at the last minute citing his "busy schedule."

2. **Trump forced Americans to recognize that our differences matter.** Knowing what does and doesn't matter to many ethnic groups is important when crafting effective messaging or building strong relationships. Creating a meaningful and engaging message can't happen by looking past race nor does looking past race make us "good Americans," better marketers, or creatives. Taking race off the table means overlooking cultural insights that could help connect with ethnic audiences on a deeper level. It robs marketers of the chance to build a strong relationship with the audience. Race and culture are often entwined. Thus, reaching specific ethnic groups requires understanding both the racial and cultural influences that play a part in shaping their decision-making process. Without this understanding, a message that seems simple and harmless can actually turn into a PR nightmare. For example, it's a big disconnect to refer to Black Americans as "the Blacks" as Trump did in a radio interview. It's similar to "you people" who, for many ethnic groups, is offensive as it is an interpretation of being ostracized.

3. **(Black) History Matters.** Failing to understand the history of an ethnic group and how it shapes their perception can lead to some major miscues. Requiring a person to submit a birth certificate or identification may seem like a reasonable request until you understand the ethnic history of the person being asked. Sherrilyn Ifill, professor at the University of Maryland School of Law, and Goldie Taylor, editor-at-large for theGrio.com, weigh in on an important history lesson that dates back to a time when Black Americans had to show papers to prove their "legitimacy." By doing so, these two authors help connect the dots from the past to today, while exposing society's "then and now" attitudes about race; they bring clarity to Trump's re-wounding of Black America.

Taylor opens her blog with the sad, emotional and real story about her great-great-grandfather that took place in 1899:

> "'Show me your papers!'
>
> "Major Blackard, then just 19 years old, dug into his trousers in search of his wallet. He patted his jacket, but could not find his billfold.
>
> ". . . he would spend the next 21 days in a cramped, musty cell. That's where his older brother Matt found him, beaten and bloodied. Matt returned with Major's employer later that day, wallet and identification card in hand, to post bond.
>
> "The so-called 'birther' movement veils a much more basic challenge to Obama's legitimacy. And yes, that challenge has a great deal to do with his race.
>
> "This is not new. Black leaders always have had to prove their 'legitimacy' and their allegiance to America. The way to smear the NAACP in the 1940s, and leaders like the Rev. Martin Luther King in the 1960s, was to suggest that they were Communists working against America."[1]

This ongoing challenge to our legitimacy is the reason that so many Blacks from earlier generations were told by our parents that we had to be smarter, more well-mannered, more well-spoken and more circumspect than our White counterparts. We had to prove ourselves worthy of the respect of Whites, and to do so required proof that we "belonged." It's among the great ironies of race in this country that when Black leaders display these same qualities, they are accused of "elitism," no matter how humble their origins.[2] How could better understanding all of this have helped Trump? We can only speculate, but Trump could have used a better understanding of this history to his advantage in two different ways:

- Stay away from the birther issue all together. After all, Trump claimed to have "a good relationship with 'the Blacks,'" why should he alienate them?

- Use this history to educate and encourage birthers to end their movement. Sure there are hard-core birthers who are never going to let it go, but by using his wealth and influence in this way, he could have helped unify the country, elevated his brand and showcased himself as a leader versus a "carnival barker" who is now losing his brand luster and followers daily.

4. **Journalism 101: Journalism's first obligation is to the truth.** Today, because of the rise of digital, news moves at a much faster pace but there are certain tenets of journalism that we have to hold onto—the truth first. Not only did the media stray from this, they also failed to verify that the information that Trump was putting forth as fact was actually fiction. Instead of behaving like the press, media became a de facto public relations channel for Trump, awarding him continuous exposure, access, and time without challenging him to substantiate his claims, all because of his wealth, privilege and America's fantasy of him as a world leader. By holding a double standard for Trump, the media was bamboozled, costing them a measure of their reputation.

The entire Donald Trump incident is more of an opportunity than a blemish for America; it gives us a reason to move the dialogue on race forward, and hopefully move our entire society closer to the ideas and principles it represents. It offers marketers the ability to learn from someone else's missteps and recognize the importance of understanding the history and culture of the group they are trying to reach.

Emotions Matter

Black people are not Vulcans.

Vulcans?

You know, Mr. Spock from *Star Trek*. He was a member of the Vulcan race, a people so one-dimensional that they have learned to suppress their emotions to the point that it seems like they don't have any. Blacks aren't Vulcans but you can't tell from their depiction in media.

Black Americans are keenly aware of how they are portrayed in the media. They realize how one-dimensional they appear in movies, TV, and advertising. Black males are painted as solemn or angry or comical, but very seldom are they seen as deep and feeling. Black women, on the other hand, are often characterized as confrontational or combative or hypersexual, but not supportive, nurturing or loving. Intentionally or not, the portrayal of Blacks in movies, TV, and advertising tends to be derived from stereotypes that are ingrained in the American culture, and not from a real knowledge or understanding of Black Americans.

In other words, Blacks are human beings, living breathing human beings with all the same emotions as any other group. And as simple and non-spectacular as this may seem, this is a huge revelation for many marketers.

PepsiCo didn't intend to offend the Black community when it aired the Pepsi Max TV spot, "Love Hurts" during the 2011 Super Bowl. Brad Bosley of Los Angeles created the ad, which was part of the Doritos and Pepsi Max Crash (a Super Bowl competition). The 28-year-old aspiring writer and director made the commercial with a budget of $800.[3]

The commercial features a Black woman rough-housing her husband in an attempt to get him to make healthier food and beverage choices. When he makes poor choices, we see her kicking him under the table at a restaurant, smashing his face into a pie, and shoving a bar of soap into his mouth.

Finally, the husband gets it. There is a scene of the husband and wife sitting on a park bench enjoying a Pepsi Max. Suddenly, he has a revelation, "good taste, zero calories," when an attractive blonde jogs by and sits down on the bench next to the husband. The jogger waves at the husband, he smiles back. The wife throws her empty can at her husband. He ducks. The can hits the girl in the head, knocking her out. As the husband and wife run off, the wife apologizes.

Good intentions were on point, but in the Black community emotions ran high about this commercial. Many comments from the Black blogosphere indicate that the spot was a reiteration of common stereotypes, and run the gamut from the angry Black women, Black couples as adversaries, to Black men being more attracted to White women than Black women, to wimpy Black men, and Black women with bad hair weaves. The discussions focused on everything but the product and it didn't position Pepsi in a positive light in the Black community. During our ca-zillionth discussion about relationships, my very close friend Marti Worell said this about the importance of positive portrayals of Black love relationships in the media:

> "Black love matters because it represents a positive picture of the Black family and our investment in it. It demonstrates that we can create and have successful families, and it shows the world what we know about these families in our community. It's so obvious that the images that go out into the world don't know us in this way. That's why Will and Jada and the Obamas are so important."

While well meaning, Pepsi failed to recognize how this spot might be received by the broader Black community, like Marti Worell, and not just mainstream consumers, its intended target. Was Pepsi being racist?

No. What it displayed with this commercial is a lack of understanding of the Black community, and how certain images might produce a negative response. Even more telling is that Pepsi is no stranger to the Black community; over the years Pepsi has had a connection with the Black community, but this is about having an understanding, about having a knowledge of the people in the community with whom a company is trying to forge a relationship.

Developing an understanding requires more than simply observing. From a distance, what is seen may not provide an accurate picture or understanding. Sometimes the only way to gain an understanding is to get up close and even participate.

The Religious Context

Consider another huge misunderstanding that society has about the Black community—religion or rather the Black church and the Black style of preaching and worshiping. From a distance some have mistaken Black worship as a show, or angry, or authoritarian. Internally, the Black community views worship as a personal and emotional relationship with God—a personal relationship that has sustained the Black community from the time during the middle passage to the present day.

In an attempt to dispel myths and stereotypes as well as to educate society about the emotional preaching styles of many Black ministers, Susan Brooks Thistlethwaite, former president of the prestigious Chicago Theological Seminary (1998–2008), and senior fellow at the Center for American Progress, wrote this *Faith Blog* post for the *Washington Post*:

> "... You cannot understand the African-American preaching tradition unless you understand the African-American church and the way in which worshipers in this tradition demand that their preachers connect with them in a deeply emotional way as an integral part of their spirituality. This is true of the prosperity gospel of Bishop T.D. Jakes or the social gospel of Rev. Dr. Jeremiah Wright.

"The deep well of suffering in slavery, in lynching, in economic deprivation and separate and unequal schools and all the other travails of the African-American experience have produced the African-American worship context. This context demands that its preachers deal with the whole of human life, its terrible trials and its unexpected miracles of triumph. And woe betide the preacher that does not address the full spectrum of truth from the pulpit in an African-American church and do so in a passionate and articulate way.

"White America, this may not be the worship context you prefer and find most spiritually uplifting. This, too, should be respected . . ."4

It is unrealistic to believe that stereotypes will fade over time by themselves; they've become ingrained into our culture and must be addressed head on. It may not be something overt. It can be as simple as creating a Black "sidekick" character that serves as comic relief, never engaging in a serious or meaningful relationship, or never displaying much depth to the character's personality.

The Entertainment Context

Despite years of popular "buddy" films and TV shows such as *I Spy* (Bill Cosby and Robert Culp), *Stir Crazy* (Richard Pryor and Gene Wilder), *Lethal Weapon* (Danny Glover and Mel Gibson), and the newest entry, *Psych* (James Roday and Dulé Hill), some Black and mainstream journalists question the validity and evolution of the relationships between these characters. To many, the Black character never gets to be fully human.

TNT's *Men of a Certain Age* (now cancelled) was an example of a television show that attempted to get it right by providing its audiences with a good dose of authentic reality. I might have skipped this show had it not been for one of my favorite actors, André Braugher, who played Owen, one of three main characters.

Owen and his two college buddies, Joe and Terry, played by Ray Romano and Scott Bakula respectively, are middle-aged and still trying to figure out the happiness equation. Owen is a bit out of shape, and lives with his wife and their three small children. He is the newly appointed president of a struggling automobile dealership that was passed on to him by his father.

I was attracted to the series because of Braugher, and quickly became a fan because of the depth of his character development. His trials and victories are equal to those of his buddies—not the same, but equal in terms of mistakes, pain and embarrassment, revelations, and the level of maturity in how he handles himself against these trials. He has health challenges, but we see him exercising, albeit often straining to keep up with his friends, but he's determined.

> **TIP:** Using emotions to create a more authentic conversation with Blacks requires understanding and balance. It isn't about being unrealistic in the messaging, but crafting a message that takes advantage of the understanding that Black people are just as emotional as any other group. After all, everybody wants to be seen as the human beings that they are, and not some one-dimensional character.

We see him struggling to please his overbearing and critical father, yet he's also a good provider and he works to validate himself through introspection and getting feedback from his friends. We see him in a healthy relationship with a loving, caring wife who is smart, strong, and supportive, not combative. Importantly, the writers did not portray Owen as "the Black friend," but as "a friend." The characters have great chemistry and are a wonderful support group for sharing their fiascos and mishaps with each other. Owen is a good friend and a good man. It is important for Black as well as mainstream audiences to see the Black man not portrayed as "the joke" or a stereotype, but an equal BFF.

Marketers must accept that it is beneficial to get emotional with Blacks in their efforts to build a richer dialogue with them. By not using as strong an emotional appeal as possible, marketers are communicating to Blacks that they do not really see or value them because they haven't taken the effort to see beyond the perception. The deeper marketers drill into the emotional gambit with Blacks, the stronger the connection becomes.

Powerful Connectors that Matter

- Demonstrating respect
- Celebration of identity, individuality, and distinctiveness
- Black romantic love
- Black men as caring caretakers
- Faith or optimism

Triggers/Disconnects

- Blacks as adversaries
- Angry Black men and women
- Use of "N-word" or ethnic slurs
- "You are so articulate"
- Referencing Black adult men or young Black men as "boy"
- Ethnic joke telling
- Speaking to Blacks in Ebonics, even if you are addressed that way.
- "Some of my best friends are Black."
- "I don't see Black when I look at you."

———

Cultural Theft

Although Boomers tend to be more sensitive about Black culture and issues surrounding race, the African-American filter spans generations. "Cultural theft" is another example of an issue that has disturbed the Black community for decades. It originates from many Blacks—young and old—who believe that Whites have benefited from trends or actions that have been created by, shaped by, or are particularly unique to Black culture. Think:

- Little Richard, Chuck Berry and rock & roll. Although Little Richard and Berry put it on the map, Elvis and Jerry Lee Lewis were credited more for its creation.

- Bo Derek's braided blonde hair style in the movie *10* (1979) became a new look for White females.
- Conservative political analyst, Pat Buchannan, who in 2009, while vehemently denouncing affirmative action on *The Rachel Maddow Show*, demonstrated total disregard and a lack of respect and recognition to the millions of Blacks who worked to provide free labor during 400 years of chattel slavery. He said (America) ". . . was built basically by White folks."
- White participation in Hip-Hop. In the film documentary, *Blacking Up*, which aired on PBS, producer Robert A. Clift explores the "tensions" surrounding this issue. Cliff writes about the dual insights that his film uncovers: "[*Blacking Up*] is an example of cultural progress—a movement toward a color-blind America. For others, it is just another case of cultural theft and mockery—a repetition of a racist past."

"Isn't imitation the highest form of flattery?" you might ask. And it may be, but not in the Black community, not always. Take Coca-Cola's 2010 National Sprite Step-Off Competition for example.

When the combined Tau and Epsilon Chapters of Zeta Tau Alpha (ZTA), a White sorority from the University of Arkansas, performed at the Step Off in Atlanta during February 2010, the mostly Black audience of Millennials cheered wildly throughout the ZTAs' performance.

However, when guest co-host Ludacris announced the ZTAs as the first place winner (which they deserved), the crowd booed, and in the Black blogosphere, some cried foul and said the decision was racist.

Apparently, there's a fine line between "cultural theft" and "imitation," and only through understanding can a marketer avoid crossing it.

Identity Matters

People of color in America are still dealing with issues of identity, self love and race head-on and daily. . . . some would like to imagine that race is a bygone issue until they have to navigate through it.

—Craig Brimm, blogger, KissMyBlackAds.com

One of my favorite videos is "I Love My Hair," created by *Sesame Street*'s head writer Jim Mazzarino. It features a dark brown Muppet character enthusiastically singing a song about why she loves her (Black) hair. Right away, you are engaged with the adorable Muppet and the lyrics she sings:

> "Don't need a trip to the beauty shop,
> 'cause I love what I got on top.
> It's curly and it's brown—and it's right up there.
> You know what I love? That's right, my hair!
> I really love my hair
> I love my hair, I love my hair.
> There's nothing else that can compare with my hair!
> I love my hair, so I must declare:
> I really, really, really love my hair!"

Mazzarino, who is White, created the video after his adopted Ethiopian daughter told him and his wife that she wanted her hair "to be long or blonde like Barbie or a princess."

It was an early sign for sure that the child was questioning her beauty, identity, and self worth through associations related to her hair.

With nearly three million views (and counting), the video is an unexpected viral success for *Sesame Street* and Mr. Mazzarino, garnering numerous interviews on national and cable news networks as well as several print and online magazine articles and blog posts.

The video is a bridge of sorts, between younger and older Blacks. Even though young Blacks have a liberated and often flamboyant outlook toward using hairstyles to create a personal statement about who they are, there is no denying the universal agreement between younger and older Blacks which is: "hair and appearance are connected with self worth and value. Mainly because it's been one of the primary reasons

African Americans have been ostracized."[5] (*See* Black Hair and Identity, *page 47*)

For the marketer trying to open or grow a dialogue with the Black community the video provides a glimpse into the importance of image and self worth to the Black community. There is a growing awareness among Blacks of images that are used to portray and speak to them.

This is important to understand because there is a tendency to think that as a society the issues of self worth and image are becoming less important, but that is not the case. Research supports the fact that the change is actually occurring at a slower rate than anyone would like.

Kenneth and Mamie Clark, legendary African-American psychologists, conducted experiments in the 1940s using dolls—one White, one Black—to gain insight on racial perspectives.

They asked Black children a variety of questions about the two dolls and found that a majority of the children—63 percent—said they'd rather play with the White doll and, in fact, favored the White doll's beauty and indicated the White doll was the better doll overall (good vs. bad).

In 2006, Kira Davis, then 17-year-old filmmaker, brought attention to the issue of racial identity and the Clarks' experiment, when she won the Diversity Award for her documentary, *A Girl Like Me*, at the Sixth Annual Media that Matters Film Festival. Davis recreated the Clarks' experiment and the results mirrored the Clarks' findings. Davis then used the insights as the framework for her documentary, which included interviews with her peers about race, skin color, and identity.

Good Morning America (*GMA*) recreated the doll test, in April 2009, among African-American girls and boys aged 5 to 9 for one of its three-part series "Black and White Now." *GMA*'s results were somewhat better than the previous experiments, yet, "the surprise," according to *GMA*, was that a majority of African-American girls said the White doll was the prettiest.

Girls in general, begin looking to validate their beauty at a young age, but African-American girls don't always find (enough) positive images of themselves in the media.

"It was revealing that young African-American girls were recognizing that the culture had identified them as Black, and not mainstream beautiful. At that time, young Black girls, particularly dark-skinned girls, rarely saw images of themselves and recognized that the media had not affirmed the gamut of Black beauty," said Najoh Tita-Reid former Associate Director of Multicultural Marketing for P&G and one of the creators of *My Black is Beautiful,* the initiative-turned-movement created to celebrate the beauty of Black women.

Many Blacks who have seen the doll test are quick to point the finger at mainstream media for promoting decades of stereotyping and other negative images, but Leonard Pitts, Jr., journalist for the *Miami Herald,* wrote about the doll tests and lambasted Black Americans for contributing to their own negative self image:

> "African Americans are, themselves, often the makers and gatekeepers. And under our aegis, the images have, in many ways, gotten worse. To surf the music video channels is to be immersed in Black culture as conceived by a new generation, a lionization of pimps and gold-diggers, hustlers and thugs who toss the N-word with a gusto that would do the Klan proud.
>
> "A new generation, afflicted with historical amnesia, blind indifference and a worship of filthy lucre, dances a metaphoric buck and wing, eyes rolling, yassuh bossing, selling itself out, selling its forebears [*sic*] out. Most of all, selling the children out."[6]

In spite of Black socio-economic progress, Black America still has issues about skin color (light skin vs. dark skin), hair (good hair vs. bad hair), and racial heritage (mixed race vs. single race).

Consider the furor that was created when it was alleged that entertainer Beyoncé Knowles's skin color was lightened in a magazine ad. The Black community immediately responded with discussions appearing both online and on national radio syndicated radio programs.

The act was seen by many as an attempt to make Beyoncé lighter as if it would make her more attractive. Whether her photo was retouched or not, the controversy that followed the ad was not what the marketer was looking for.

Filmmaker Bill Duke explores the biased attitudes about skin color among the Black community in his new documentary, *Dark Girls*. Duke uses several clips from interviews of dark-skinned Black women who share their stories and pain of being ostracized and demeaned by family, friends, and others in the Black community based on their skin color. One woman talks about how, as a child, she wanted to use a little bleach in her bath hopeful that it would lighten her skin; another talked of being taunted, teased, and called "tar baby" by her Black peers.

Sherry, an attractive manager for an insurance company, confessed that she was willing to broaden her dating options to include White males. When she reviewed profiles of potential White males, very few mentioned Black women as a dating option. High on the list were White females, Asian women, and "exotic Asian and Latino women"—all of which have become mainstream's new standard of beauty.

The reality is the struggle of having to think about one's identity is still very real for people of color. From biracial Blacks who are often pressured to "choose and declare" and the few students of color who find themselves in the midst of a majority White student population, identity matters. The need to consciously or unconsciously think, "Black first" is often equated with fighting the myth that being Black has less value than other races or cultures.

Touré, author, journalist, and MSNBC contributor, writes with astute insight, clarity, and wisdom about what Blackness means in his recent book, *Who's Afraid of Post-Blackness? What It Means to Be Black Now* (Free Press, 2011). In one chapter, the author uses bold examples to tell the stories about the Black community's response from the self-inflected burdens from Black American's "Black Gaze," in which Blacks are measured by other Blacks by the degree of their Blackness. In other words, "Are they Black enough?" and the unspoken obligation for

Blacks to bring the Black community along and not shame them in the process.

Touré writes of White American's "White Gaze," society's embrace of Black stereotypes and the belief that Black anything—Black experience, Black neighborhoods, Black education, Black consumers, Black ad agencies, Black marketing, Black men, Black women, Black children—or a Black President—has little or no value.

"People of color understand that identity and self-love problems are things they have to work out," says Craig Brimm, owner/blogger of *KissMyBlackAds.com*. For example, Black parents want their children to be fully engaged and immersed in the diversity of America, yet most also want their children to have Black role models.[7]

"Identity is tied to what we believe about ourselves. It took me years to find my identity," says Stedman Graham author of *Identity: Passport to Freedom*, one of many books from his "Nine Steps to Success" series and personal development program. Graham takes his Identity Passport-design booklet primarily to students—especially to African-American and Latino students, and opens his workshops and presentations with the question, "What happens when you don't have an identity?" Graham has been a warrior for identity development since 1997. It's personal.

Graham gives further details about his passion for this program during an interview:

> "Too many of these kids define themselves by the outside world in terms of race, religion, money and jobs and need to better connect with themselves—which the system doesn't teach us.
>
> "My goal is to educate as many of these kids as possible about how to develop an identity for themselves, help them find out who they are, and make the information relevant to their own development."

Media and communications companies as creators and gatekeepers of images, have an opportunity to effectively connect with Black Americans in a positive and compelling way by creating messages and initiatives that demonstrate an appreciation for our differences—particularly around identity—instead of pretending they don't exist or ignoring them. The issue of image like skin color is more than Black or White. It covers a spectrum of shades, but if a marketer is going to successfully make a connection with the Black community, they must first understand that image is an issue that has to be understood and addressed.

Black Hair and Identity

Black women spare no expense when it comes to their hair. Given society's intrigue with Black hair, the Black community's frequent judgment about Black hair, and all the challenges associated with styling and maintaining their hair, Black women are likely to spend two to three times as much money on their hair as White females.

Hair weaving—the process of adding human or synthetic hair to existing hair via braiding, sewing, or gluing—has literally exploded. At prices ranging from $350 to over $1,500, many Black women are selling their souls for this hairstyle. "It's got to be 60–70% of Black women wearing weaves," says master barber/stylist, Leoma Johns. Johns does not perform the process (yet) but has a number of stylists in her Chicago-based South Loop salon that do.

Johns's estimates may not be too far off. Industry stats indicate that the hair weaving business makes up about 65% of the hair-care revenue with the majority of those dollars coming from Black women.[8] Black women see weaves as extensions of themselves and say the longer hair styles are more about style options and feeling feminine. In addition to providing style versatility, long hair provides an equalizer for men and society who identify long hair as the standard of beauty.

Dotty, a college student, who wears her hair in a short natural hairstyle, shares her experience with different hairstyles and confirms this finding:

"I've worn a lot of different hairstyles; natural hair, short Afro, big Afro, relaxed hair, but the most positive attention I received was when I had my long hair weave. I got a lot of attention from people in general, but the most came from men. Black men say they like Black women with natural hair, or short hair, but the long hair got 'em every time."

Lindsey, a corporate manager, shares concerns about the possible fall out from changing from her weaved style to her natural hair:

"My White colleagues definitely like my hair long and straight like theirs. I want to change my style to give my hair a break, but am concerned about whether something as insignificant as my hair would cause a problem with me getting a promotion."

Chris Rock uses comedy to explore the hair weaving phenomenon and Black women's obsession with it in his 2010 documentary, *Good Hair*. I was particularly drawn to one woman who wanted to get rid of her weave but was concerned about her husband's reaction (and possible rejection). She had the weave when they met and had it throughout their 7-year marriage. Her husband had never seen her natural hair. I also shook my head with despair at the women, all of them celebrities, who admitted that they did not exercise because they didn't want to ruin their weaved hairstyles. This rationale is a common barrier to exercise and a factor related to poor health among Black women.

At the same time, natural styles are moving to new heights. Those who engage in wearing natural styles say they are making a personal style statement, celebrating their culture, or, among a few, making a political statement.

"Natural hair is not only a commitment to look good but is a commitment to a lifestyle choice a political choice and cultural choice. It's more than just a style."

—African-American female focus group respondent and
natural hair style wearer

Yet, for Lindsey, the corporate manager and some others, African-American hair styles are still causing job-related issues:

"This summer while traveling on an international flight, a fiftyish African-American flight attendant knelt down next to my aisle seat to ask questions about my natural hair. In addition to my hairstyle catching her eye, she was drawn to me (she said) because she noticed that I was working feverishly on my laptop. She wanted to know what business I was in and how well my colleagues responded to my hairstyle. She mentioned that she recently changed her hair style from relaxed and straight to a short natural style and was getting flack from her non-Black superiors."

In Rock's film, a group of young Black women, wearing straight hairstyles, critique a peer's unstructured natural style. They say to the woman and the interviewer that her hair style would be a barrier for hiring as well as promotions because no one "would take her seriously."

Two years ago, in response to Black consumers' complaints about negative images in the media, we tracked the roles of Black characters in TV commercials for eight months. One of our discoveries was that in roughly 8 out of 10 commercials, Black women wore natural hairstyles. This most likely was in response to criticism by African Americans who believe images of Black beauty were closer to those of mainstream beauty. Using the "natural hair factor" is one way of celebrating Black beauty. Using Black models with natural hair also makes a statement about inclusion—that this is a person of color (i.e., from African descent).

The bottom line is that unfiltered acceptance is very important to African Americans and their hair plays a (big) role in positive recognition.

———

Isn't She Lovely?
Absolutely! Says Procter & Gamble's
My Black is Beautiful Initiative

Kisha Mitchell Williams, multicultural brand manager, and Pamela Rhett, assistant multicultural brand manager, know the answer. No matter the size, shape, skin-tone or sensibilities, their quest helps woman of color shout, *"My Black is Beautiful!"* Procter & Gamble, their employer, joined the women's vision and co-signed their plan. *My Black is Beautiful!* creates opportunities for African American women to realize and proclaim their loveliness, inside and out. *My Black is Beautiful* ensures that women on both sides of the P&G

counter can contribute by expressing their thoughts about the images and products presented. The norms of Black women become the norms presented in the national and global arenas through this partnership.

My Black is Beautiful is a BET television show, a website, a multi-city tour and dialogues held across the country that create occasions to educate and inspire women of color. Using P&G brands (Pantene Relaxed & Natural, Cover Girl Queen Collection, Olay Definity, Crest Pro-Health, Tampax, Always, and Clairol Beautiful Collection) and spokeswomen, *My Black Is Beautiful* connects African-American women to resources and ideas for maintaining and improving their physical, mental and spiritual selves in a supportive, non-judgmental environment. Through the *My Black Is Beautiful* website, women can arrange for discussion groups and events to continue to expand the movement. The initiative has a page on Facebook and generates an email newsletter, providing resources that reach the younger segment of this population.

TIP: Not all programs or advertising need be serious or sappy, but the question *How does this idea add value?* should be an important component of marketing strategy development when targeting Blacks and other underserved segments.

First partnering with *Essence* magazine to create the website discussion guides, MBIB is now an official sponsor of the Essence Music Festival and will present demonstrations and consultations for those who attend. The original program has extended to incorporate *My Home Made Beautiful* which supports women in making their physical surroundings places of beauty and comfort.

One tangible benefit of the *My Black Is Beautiful* initiative for Procter & Gamble is assistance in recruiting minority candidates for the company. However, of value to both P&G and the African-American female consumer is P&G's invitation to exchange "secrets" with the consumer. Procter & Gamble will show Black women how to use their products to attain and sustain things that matter—their health, their spirit, their homes, their relationships in a way that expresses and enhances the true beauty of an African-American woman without compromising her values and her vision. In turn, the consumer receives products designed and promoted with her in mind.9

Notes

1. Goldie Taylor, "Why Obama Shouldn't Have to Show His Papers," *www.theGrio.com,* April 28, 2011.

2. Sherrilyn Ifill, "It's Not about His Birth, It's about His Race," www.cnn.com, April 28, 2011.

3. *Los Angeles Times,* Show Tracker, February 6, 2011.

4. Susan Brooks Thistlethwaite, "Memo to White America: Respect African-American Preaching," *Washington Post* online, April 26, 2008.

5. Craig Brimm, "10 Things Marketers Can Learn from a Muppet," *www.KissMyBlackAds.com,* October 21, 2010.

6. Leonard J. Pitts, "Blacks Often Share Blame for Poor Self-image," *Miami Herald,* September 18, 2006.

7. Yankelovich and Associates/Radio One, *Black America Today Study,* 2008.

8. Alene Dawson, "Hair in the Black community: Roots of a Debate," www.latimes.com, October 11, 2009.

9. www.myBlackisbeautiful.com.

CHAPTER 4

Black Gold:
Finding the Mother Lode Hidden in Plain Sight

Imagine waking up each day, and from the second you leave your home everywhere you go there is gold just lying around waiting to be picked up and yet you just walk on by. Gold is everywhere you go (work, stores and malls, restaurants, movies, school, the park)—it is everywhere, and still you walk right past it, never stopping to pick up a nugget. You barely even look at as you go about your day.

"Impossible," you say.

Yet, despite the growth of the Black population and its trillion dollar plus spending power, marketers ignore or take for granted the patronage of their businesses by Blacks. They're ignoring a potential gold rush of customers. However, the growing affluence of Blacks is stimulating demand for a variety of products and services not traditionally linked to the Black community that is hard to ignore. Here are some examples of increased demand among Blacks:

- In 2009, new and used car sales were up 22% and 37% respectively from 2007.[1]

- There have been significant gains in U.S. and International travel by Blacks who spend more than $5 billion annually on travel.[2]

- Blacks are more likely to be early adapters of new technologies. They are more likely to own a smartphone (31% vs. 27% for Whites),[3] and their spending for computers and peripherals was up 171%[4] in 2009 over 2007.

- There is an increasing demand for books written by Black authors featuring Black characters.

- Annual expenditures by African-Americans on health and beauty aids are estimated at around $9 billion because looking good is a priority for many African Americans. How one looks is a powerful statement of what one is "all about."

- Although 17.5% of African Americans are unbanked or under-banked, this segment provides opportunities for new financial products and services that can serve people where they are.

Nonetheless, as these industries continue to search for bigger ideas and opportunities, the Black community continues to be underserved. They continue to ignore the gold waiting to be mined due to either a false perception or a lack of understanding.

Let's look at a few of the gold fields that aren't being mined despite proven growth and desire.

Reading Between the Lines—the Power of Black Book Readers

"I went to school with Dick and Jane, and Beatrix Potter, whom I loved, but when did I ever see my picture? Never," says Joyce Dinkins, an African American and managing editor of New Hope Publishers. "Say you had a taste for blueberry lemonade, and you waited years and years for someone to make it, and then finally somebody did and you tasted it. You wouldn't be able to get enough of it, and you'd tell all your friends. It's pent up demand."[5]

One of the most perturbing and long-standing myths about Black folks is "If you want to hide information from the Black community, put it in a book." Unfortunately, both Blacks and non-Blacks take this myth to heart.

For years, fiction that featured Black characters was nearly an underground phenomenon, limited only to the Black community. Then, Terry McMillan, who was popular among Black women but not as well known to mainstream readers, became famous when two of her novels, *Waiting to Exhale* and *How Stella Got Her Groove Back,* became blockbuster movies.

Importantly, McMillan's success demonstrated to the publishing world that there was a market for Black fiction.

Before *Exhale* and *Stella,* demand for African-American books was on the rise but unnoticed by mainstream publishers. Between 1992 and 2000 sales doubled, and there was a 14.8 percent increase in purchases after *Exhale* (1995). Sales continue to rise. These book buyers tend to be mostly females aged 18 to 55 who buy books for themselves, for their children, and as gifts for others. Particularly, they want books that speak to their life experiences.

Thus, the growing Black interest in Black books has fueled growth in niche books, Black book clubs as well as relevant businesses and publications:

- In 1999, Doubleday Direct launched Black Expressions. Promoting books for and by African Americans, it boasted that 40,000 members had joined in less than six months. By 2008, Carol Mackey, Black Expressions' editor-in-chief, announced that the online retailer and direct marketer of general interest and specialty book clubs for Black readers had more than 350,000 members, 95% of whom are African-American women.[6]

- With over 900,000 unique visitors per month, The African-American Literature Book Club (AALBC.com) is a massive site that is not a "club" but a widely recognized source of author profiles, book recommendations, intriguing online discussion boards, writer's resources, articles, and critical reviews of books by and about African Americans.

- North Paran, a website dedicated to books by and about Black people, was formed with an eye toward philanthropy. Its goal is to get a book in the hands of every child in the Black community who doesn't have one. North Paran partners with non-profit organizations in the United States and abroad to find children who do not have access to new books, and donates a new book to a child in need for every book sold on its site.

- Then there's Pam Perry. She's a successful book publicity coach targeting Black authors—particularly Black Christian authors—and is relentless about promoting her authors and her business via a variety of media. Perry has tapped into a niche that big businesses and large publishers ignored, and what a "mother lode" she has found.

  Perry, through her company, Ministry Marketing Solutions, uses social media, online radio and TV platforms, blogs, and videos to connect with more than 500,000 people, which includes authors and their audiences. If you're on her email list, you're going hear from her at least once a week with some big announcement or get some free useful information. I don't dare remove her, because I'm afraid I might miss something important. And I would.

- According to *Publishers Weekly*, African-American Christian fiction exploded onto the publishing scene in 1997 when former literary agent Denise Stinson launched Walk Worthy Press based on her own desire to read stories she couldn't find anywhere else—namely, fiction featuring African-American characters who encountered real-world struggles and triumphs, with a righteous twist.[7]

- Benefiting from all these efforts are Black book club members like Gwen Kelly and Angie Powell. They are two of thousands of active Black book club members across the United States. Although both are very busy, Gwen took the time to start an online book club via Facebook, and Angie flies from Chicago to Dallas once per quarter, to participate in her book club gathering.

- One big problem: "Black authors want their books in Black bookstores, be it brick-and-mortar or online, but mainstream publishers aren't aware of these retailers," says Barbara Kensey, president of Kensey and Kensey Communications, a public relations firm in Chicago. "The other challenge is getting publishers to understand the different niche segments of Black readers and the opportunities to reach them." Kensey further explains, "One of my authors, Dr. Lawrence Jackson, wrote *The Indignant Generation,* a narrative history of the neglected but essential history of African-American writers and critics between The Harlem Renaissance (1934) and Civil Rights (1960). The book is priced at $35. His publisher squabbled a bit when it learned that Kensey and the author wanted to take the book to the Black community. "That price tag and topic will never sell they told us," said Kensey. "We know our audience, so we scheduled the book signings and sold out every time!"

Tapping into Black America's book reading and book retail interests is another way to connect with them in a culturally relevant way.

Marketers should consider partnering with online African-American booksellers and resources via advertisements, coupons, sales, and product sampling. Aligning with these high traffic businesses with desirable audience demos would be beneficial to companies and organizations that are seeking to establish a credible relationship with Black Americans.

Avid Black readers are one of many opportunities waiting to be properly mined by marketers, but until marketers can recognize and understand the treasure that Black consumers represent these fields will remain untapped.

"Black People Love Their Rides"

The title above from MultiCultClassics' blog (multicultclassics.blogspot. com) has never been more true.

For most people, next to the purchase of a home, automobiles are one of the biggest, most important purchases in their lifetimes. Americans in general have a unique affinity for automobiles. Muscle cars, convertibles, off-road vehicles, sports cars, luxury sedans, and so forth—a lot of how Americans want to be viewed is reflected in the types of vehicles they drive.

In the African-American community this feeling is even stronger. For many, automobiles often serve as "badge value"—in that they are a means for creating or confirming how they want to be perceived. Although there are plenty of songs about cars in all types of American music, an excerpt from Will Smith's 1990s "Summertime" hit encapsulates "badge value," and how many African Americans feel about their cars:

Then six 'o clock rolls around
You just finished wipin' your car down
It's time to cruise so you head to the summertime hangout
it looks like a car show
Everybody come lookin' real fine
Fresh from the barber shop or fly from the beauty salon
Every moment frontin' and maxin'
Chillin' in the car they spent all day waxin'
Leanin' to the side but you can't speed through
Two miles an hour so, everybody sees you . . .[8]

According to findings from Strategic Visions' African-American automotive study, African Americans show a distinctive emotional profile on key aspects of the "super values" (Security, Freedom, Esteem, and Balance) that make up the experience owners have with their vehicles.

While "badge value" is not the only reason for purchasing a specific vehicle, for many African Americans it is one of the stronger factors. How and why this happens? We can only speculate but stepping out into the world in brown skin means going up against negative stereotypes, and possibly for African Americans, a vehicle is one of the mechanisms for combating the negative perceptions or it can be a means of self expression. Whatever the reason, this is an important cultural insight that continues to be ignored or tossed to the side as "been there, done that" trivia.

However, if automobile manufacturers had been there and done that, they would still be doing it. The numbers for automobile sales in the African-American community are hard to ignore.

In 2010, in the midst of the economic downturn, the African-American market volume was 68.6 percent greater than the non-ethnic market, or 10 times greater than general market within the time period, according to R.L. Polk, a premier provider of automotive information and marketing solutions.

The Polk study also revealed that in 2010 the top five brands accounted for 60 percent of the African-American market, each with more than a 10 percent share. Toyota leads the top 10 brands with a 15 percent share, followed by Ford (11.7%) and then Chevrolet (11.4%). These brands that enjoy double-digit market share with Black consumers, also invest in the Black consumer market.[9]

"With the U.S. population growing faster in the African-American segment than others, there's a significant opportunity for automotive manufacturers and dealers to begin to align marketing initiatives toward this specific audience," said Marc Bland, product strategist at Polk.

Following are successful programs from the top two—Toyota and Ford.

Toyota

Burrell Communications has had the Toyota business since 2004. Its work has primarily been with cars, but recently, they picked up the RAV4, Toyota's smaller SUV.

Burrell's V.P. and associate director of account planning, Kevin Brockenbrough, had a lot to say about Toyota's successful relationship with the African-American community.

Mr. Brockenbrough's answers were so thoughtful, that I felt it best to print his responses to the interview as he presented them to me. That interview follows:

Miller: What makes Toyota #1 with Blacks (vs. others)?

Brockenbrough: There's a quote that I think sums up what makes Toyota successful with Blacks:

"We're attracted to what reminds us of ourselves."

That comes from Dan Hill's book on emotionally effective advertising, *About Face* (Kagen Page, 2010). But I think it captures the essence of the relationship between Toyota and its African-American consumers. When Black consumers think of Toyota, they use the same words they'd use to describe themselves: dependable, reliable, hard-working, smart, stylish (but in an understated way), more than meets the eye, surprising—"you think you know me, but you don't."

I think that in life, you look at a person's track record. When you pick someone out to be your friend, you pick a person that shares your values and approaches life the same way you do. I think the same is true of the products we buy. We buy products that share our values. Our products tell a lot about us, and driving a Toyota says that I'm a person you can depend on and one that makes smart decisions.

I also think that we enter into relationships with the products we buy. We want them to be reliable and drama free. We rush to tell our friends when our favorite products do things that surprise and delight us. You hear that about both Toyota and Lexus.

It's the commitment to getting the little things right that keeps you coming back. There are a lot of good-looking cars on the road but they don't have Toyota's track record. You don't hear stories of people buying Toyotas and being disappointed with them like you do with other manufacturers. Blacks trust Toyota. And trust is a very precious thing in the Black community. It has to be earned.

Miller: How Did Burrell, if at all, play a part in this? What ads/ad messages worked well with the Black community and what in particular made them effective?

Brockenbrough: In the world of marketing, everybody's concerned about ROI—return on investment. The manufacturer is thinking about it. The dealer is thinking about it. Even the buyer of the car is thinking about it.

But I think Tom Burrell started this shop with a different definition of ROI. For us, ROI stands for Realism, Optimism, and Insight. I think there's a commitment at Burrell to showing realistic portrayals of African Americans. It starts with our researchers working with Toyota's research department to make sure we know who we're talking to and that we get the motivation right and we get the message right. An example is the new work we've done on Toyota's Prius hybrid. We'd never done any ads for Prius before, so Toyota let us go out and do a lot of exploratory research to find out what people knew—and more importantly, didn't know—about hybrid cars. Blacks loved the gas mileage but one of their biggest concerns was "What will my friends think of me if I buy a Prius?"

So we built an ad that has a couple preparing to go to a college homecoming—a place where they're sure to see lots of friends—and they get to the rental company and the car they're given is a Prius. The driver—a Black man—immediately shows the same worry we heard in our research: he's worried about what people will think about him if he pulls up in a Prius. That's the "R" in our ROI formula: focusing on what's "REAL."

But his wife demonstrates the "O" in our ROI formula: Optimism. She thinks it will be fine ("I think it's cute.") and encourages him to get in and experience it for himself versus worrying what other people will think.

And that leads us to the "I" in our ROI formula: Insight. The key problem for Prius was that it was unfamiliar. So how do you sell the unfamiliar? You sell the unfamiliar with the familiar: family, friends, and personal experience.

His wife invites the driver (her husband, and indeed, all of us) to give the Prius a try. It's a rental, so he's basically getting an extended test drive. He gets to familiarize himself with the car without any pressure from any salesman. At the college homecoming, we see a friend climbing inside the Prius and also checking it out. The driver's wife likes it. He likes it. His friends like it. Sold! "Hey, we're getting one of these . . . "

Miller: Are there any targeted campaigns that helped increase sales or awareness of a particular Toyota vehicle?

Brockenbrough: The Prius campaign I just mentioned has generated a 97 percent increase in sales vs. a year ago (YAG) among African-American buyers. It's also growing at a faster rate than total market sales of Prius (which are up 77%). We also have a brand experience—The Toyota Green Initiative—happening on Black college campuses designed to further educate the Black community on how to live green. Many of our Black leaders come out of Historically Black Colleges and Universities and those students are active in leading change in the communities they call "home." We wanted to give them the tools to help their friends and families "go green."

Miller: Any Black insights related to Toyota that you can share?

Brockenbrough: We have to sell the sheet metal, but it's also important to celebrate the driver. I think that's particularly true with Black customers. You want to give them good information about the vehicle but always portray the driver as being smart enough to make his or her own decision.

I also think you have to be sensitive to the images you portray on screen. We show a husband and wife. We don't show a Black woman bossing around her man and we don't show a Black man unwilling to listen to his wife. We show the impact that family and friends can have on the buying decision but put the driver in a position to make up his own mind. It may not seem important from the outside looking in, but when you think of this culture's history as slaves, Blacks are very sensitive to having someone else make decisions for them. Especially Black men. And we don't show the Black man as the butt of the joke like you see in so many ads today. We show him as smart and caring—and viewers can infer that Toyota is the same way.

Miller: What is it about Burrell's Toyota campaign(s) that resonated with African Americans?

Brockenbrough: Familiarity mixed with surprise. Comments like:

"Yeah, that's me. I could definitely see myself doing that."

"I have a family member who acts (or talks) just like that."

We show both familiar situations and familiar characters in a way that feels real, but still feels fresh. That sounds simple but it's not. Familiar can sometimes lead to "Oh, I've seen that before." Whatever you serve up has to be both culturally relevant and creatively engaging, so you've got to put a spin on the familiar so that it feels new.

We've been successful in showing Toyota's products in ways that make Black consumers think differently about Toyota while showing the Black driver as a hero. For example, we got strong response from Black men to a Camry line ad directed at Black women. It highlighted the many roles Black women play (executives, housewives, and girls having a night on the town). The ad spoke to the safety enhancements in Camry and had a line that said, "Even heroes need protecting." Black men liked the fact that Toyota would salute their women that way. And that Camry campaign beat its sales goal by 22 percent, and awareness for Camry among Black women rose by 17 percent.

Ford: The "All-In" Campaign

Ford has had a long-term relationship with the Black community and continues to pull out all the stops to connect with them. Its targeted efforts are paying off.

In 2010 Ford launched the "All-In" campaign which showcases high-ranking African-American executives at Ford. Through print, radio and digital executions, and a series of web videos, these executives discuss Ford's successful turn-around plan via its respective leadership positions in the areas of quality, technology, the environment, and community relations.

"All In" has been very successful in helping Ford effectively connect with the Black community," says Marc Perry, Group Account Director at the UniWorld Group, the ethnic agency for Ford.

"Ford cares about the African-American community and understands the importance of balancing the landscape both in and outside of Ford with positive African-American images, so the big turn-around stories were led by these executives. This approach helped African Americans feel a genuine connection to the brand," Perry adds.

Fiesta Movement

UniWorld created a casting call event where five of the most uniquely stylish individuals appear in a national advertisement for the 2011 Fiesta. To promote this event and the Fiesta, UniWorld created "The Fiesta Movement" social media initiative. It generated huge buzz with more than 6.2 million YouTube views, more than 750,000 Flickr views, and nearly 4 million Twitter impressions. Most importantly, more than 100,000 people expressed an earlier interest in the 2011 Ford Fiesta.

Celebrity Endorsements Matter

Consumers often claim during focus groups that celebrities don't matter, but that is during a focus group where people can sometimes craft their responses to match what they think is the correct answer instead of answering honestly. However, away from the focus groups in homes across America, the right celebrities matter a lot. The right celebrities can attract attention to the brand, increase awareness, and if really good, motivate consumers towards purchase consideration.

Autoblog.com ranks "Crazy Kevin," Ford's Explorer commercial featuring Kevin Hart, a "B." But Hart, an African-American comedian and actor who has starred in several films including, the *Scary Movie* sequels, *Little Fockers*, and *The 40-Year-Old Virgin*, has amazing social media exposure and connections. He has a million plus followers on Twitter, nearly 5,000 Facebook friends, and millions of viewers who have checked out his stand-up routines on YouTube. All of which earns him an "A" as an influential celebrity for the Ford brand.

UniWorld's "Crazy Kevin" campaign consists of TV ads, print, radio and digital executions and features Hart showing up late for his brother's wedding in a 2011 Ford Explorer. The campaign engages its audience with Hart's wild comedic antics, as he hits key product features hard like the unique Terrain Management System, and rear inflatable seatbelts.

In fact, some among "Crazy Kevin's" 45,000 YouTube viewers admit to buying or wanting to buy the 2011 Explorer as a result of this ad. The campaign debuted on BET and ran on TV One, and was so successful that it was expanded to general market audiences as well, including the 2011 NBA All-Star Game.

We have to be inclusive. We are a niche marketer in many ways. . . .
African American is an important part of that too . . . it's something
that I think we have to take a serious look at, and not just lip service,
but that's going to help us grow.

—Tim Mahoney, EVP and chief product & marketing officer for
Volkswagen of America at The Rainbow Push 12th Annual
Global Automotive Summit, in Detroit, October 2011[10]

Top Automotive Brands[11]

- Buick, Hyundai, Kia, Cadillac, GMC and Infiniti are doing extremely well with the African-American market. With the exception of Cadillac, all grew faster in 2010 within the African-American market versus the overall market.

- Buick and Hyundai led with large gains in new car registrations in the African-American market. In 2010 Buick was up by 72.2% and Hyundai registrations increased by 53.2% over 2009 registrations.

- According to Diversity Affluence,[12] luxury sedans are the most common current and future vehicle types preferred by African Americans. In fact, those who own mid-range and economy vehicles are looking to trade up in their next purchase or lease to a more prestigious option.

The Top 10 Automotive Brands among African-American Car Buyers

1.	Toyota	15.0%
2.	Ford	11.7
3.	Chevrolet	11.4
4.	Honda	11.3
5.	Nissan	10.2
6.	Hyundai	5.6
7.	Kia	4.2
8.	Dodge	4.0
9.	GMC	2.8
10.	Volkswagen	2.2

Source: *Polk Company News*, April 26, 2011

Travel: African Americans Getting Out and Seeing the World

When you are Black and venture somewhere exotic, there is always a deeper feeling of accomplishment, and the experience is all the richer when you share it with folks that come from a similar background. You can't help but have an incredible feeling of euphoria for how far you had to come to get to that point.

—Jose Jones, founder, National Black Scuba Divers

African Americans are taking their fun on the road, heading out to distant destinations in search of new and exciting travels and adventures. And they're bringing their friends along.

Black travel and tourism is a $40 billion industry. Today's Black traveler is more savvy than ever, breaking out of the typical vacation habits in search of a more enriching experience. Many who were once likely to drive within the contiguous states are now seeking "Black friendly" spots like Mexico and the Caribbean. While those who have been enjoying "sun and beach" vacations are raising the bar by exploring a variety of places worldwide including Africa, Brazil, Europe, and Asia.

African-American travel is big business, made even bigger because they are traveling in groups.

African Americans tend to enjoy traveling in groups, and connecting and meeting up with other Black travelers worldwide. Many are also seeking out travel clubs run by and for Black travelers. Besides Black ski clubs, there are travel clubs for Black scuba divers, golfers, boaters and more.

"If you're new to skiing, it's different learning it in a Black group, you get a lot more nurturing," said one traveler.[13]

Alvin (Al) Alassane Jackson and his long-time sweetheart JoAnn (Jo) Jackson have traveled the world and Al has the art, artifacts, and photos to share with his guests: a huge wall hanging from Senegal, a tiny statue from Australia, or an interesting something-or-other from Austria. Al has a story to tell about each item. Bragging rights—in such a good way.

Al and Jo don't always take these excursions alone. They are also members of a national Black Ski organization that includes hundreds of Black ski clubs across America, and holds ski summits all over the world.

Some veteran Black skiers explain that they started their own groups because they did not feel welcomed at several predominately White ski resorts. However, for younger skiers, traveling in groups was less about racial discrimination and more about lifestyle:

> "When traveling alone or in small groups to these places, we stand out. . . . We were treated courteously, but the atmosphere was kinda stiff. Even though I did not feel a sense of being genuinely welcomed, I didn't feel unwelcome either, and thought, 'This is a nice place, so why not bring our own party—our own flava'. So we did and it was really cool for us," says Jill, a young Millennial traveler.

Al counters the veteran skier comments by candidly pointing to the economic benefits that Black skiers bring to several exclusive venues and ski communities:

> "Thousands of Black skiers would descend on these small towns, and spend lots of money. They'd shop for fashions, jewelry, and groceries. They were dining out, and drinking premium liquor. Their presence had a tremendously positive economic impact on everything. White people wanted to hang out with us, party with us and often asked, 'When are you guys coming back?'"

Al is also passionate about African Americans understanding their history about the Black Diaspora (the dispersion of Africans throughout the world as a result of those who were enslaved), the impact of the slave trade, and often organizes trips with small groups to West Africa, South Africa, and Bahia, Brazil. Many Black churches share the same passion as Al. It is common for Trinity UCC in Chicago, T.D. Jakes's Potter's House, or Abyssinian in New York City (among others), to organize three or more sojourns of 40 to 100+ people per year to these same places. For many African Americans, it's their first international trip and following this trip they feel more encouraged to venture to other global destinations. One mega-church sojourner told me: "I went to Africa first, out of respect. Now I'm ready to see the rest of the world."

Blacks and cruise vacations

There is a running joke in the Black community about Blacks and cruise vacations: Why don't you see Black folks on cruise ships? Because they fell for that trick once before.

The myth within the joke—that Black Americans don't cruise—at one time may have had some validity. Years ago, travel research revealed that a disproportionate number of African Americans believed that cruise vacations were not a safe option. But the biggest barrier to Blacks and cruise vacations was that no company had extended an invitation—until Royal Caribbean Cruise Lines.

Just 12 years ago there was a chasm between African Americans and Royal Caribbean International (RCCL). I recall working on the pitch with the Chisholm-Mingo ad agency, helping them win the business and then diving into focus groups for the brand.

In group after group, among respondents who either had experience with cruise travel or those who had not, but were intending to take a cruise vacation, one thing was common—most felt unwelcome by Royal Caribbean. Respondents commented that cruise themes were not relevant to their lifestyle, (perceived) unfriendly ship guests who didn't look like them, and they pointed to advertising that didn't include them.

But former senior VP Dan Hanrahan repositioned the Royal Caribbean brand to appeal to a broader, more active consumer market via the acclaimed "Get Out There" campaign, which introduced millions of people to cruising. Additionally and importantly, a position for the head of multicultural markets was also created, which meant there was someone in charge of African-American markets who invested in research and a fully integrated ad campaign that targeted African Americans.

The results of Royal Caribbean investing in the Black traveler yielded a number of chartered cruises and themed interest cruises including: family cruises, single cruises, gospel cruises, business cruises, hair style cruises, jazz cruises, college cruises, and many more.

One of Royal Caribbean's most popular and successful cruises is Tom Joyner's Fantastic Voyage. For eleven years, nationally-syndicated DJ Tom Joyner has chartered one of Royal Caribbean's ships through the Tom Joyner Foundation to raise money for Historically Black Colleges and Universities (HBCUs). Named the "Fantastic Voyage," the results have been exactly that—fantastic! Cruises sell out in days, and many cruisers have become repeat travelers with RCCL.

At the height of its popularity, there was even talk of chartering two ships to match demand. Even through the "economic turndown" the cruise has been a success.

Today, more than 30 percent of African Americans are taking cruise vacations, versus a significantly lower number 15 years ago. It's a way for them to travel in groups, and visit different locations within one trip. It took the efforts of one company to help showcase the value of the Black cruise traveler.

And although travel industry statistics reflect increased numbers of Black cruisers long before the Fantastic Voyage, the Joyner/RCCL partnership should be credited with encouraging and influencing a large number of Blacks to consider cruise vacations.

There are a number of Black travel information websites, travel clubs and bloggers that foster Black travel connectivity. These sites and groups provide additional opportunities for marketers to connect with Black America, and many welcome the opportunity to have sponsors develop an up close unique relationship with the Black traveler. Being part of their travels can lead marketers to discover untapped opportunities.

By the Numbers

Survey Highlights from 2011 African-American Travel Conference

The African-American Travel Conference (AATC) an association of 2,500 travel planners, serving the African-American community conducted a survey among its travel planners in 2011 and learned:

88% are finding new travelers in the Black community

New travelers who use a travel agent tend to be older:

age	45	11%
	46 to 50	15%
	51 to 55	19%
	56 to 60	37%
	60+	18%

66% are planning international tours

63% say Black travelers are traveling by air

60% are booking 3-star accommodations

31% are booking 4-star accommodations

66% say Black travelers have taken a cruise

American Airlines: Black Atlas[SM]

Black Atlas, created by American Airlines, is a comprehensive, informative website where African American, or any other, traveler can find or share information on points of interest in major Black cities nationally and internationally. Traveler/members have posted items on over 70 international cities from Accra to Zurich, and on many domestic locations as well.

Launched in October 2009, Black Atlas is a wealth of tips and tidbits on destinations, itinerary building, and best fares. Articles and updates, focusing on locations of importance to African-American vacationers are all here. To find the best barbershop in Barcelona or the coolest jazz radio station in Dallas, travelers are invited to check Black Atlas. Everyday travelers, and experts, like editor-at-large, Nelson George are found on Black Atlas. Travelers are also invited to become members and post their own reviews and travel videos or recommend spots worth visiting in their favorite cities.

The Black Atlas site showcases upcoming events and festivals in major African-American destinations. News is frequently updated to be of greatest value to today's Black vacationer, world traveler or family reunion celebrator.

————

Notes

1. "The Buying Power of Black Americans," *Target Market News*, 2009.
2. Ibid.
3. *Nielsen Wire*, February 1, 2011.
4. "Buying Power," op. cit.
5. Angie Kiesling, "African American Market Comes of Age," *Publishers Weekly*, September 1, 2008.
6. Ibid.
7. Ibid.
8. "Summertime," lyrics performed by Will Smith, written by Paul Taylor, Mats Olof Yummell, and Magnus Lars Eklund. Used by permission.
9. "Toyota Top Choice among African-American Car Buyers in 2010," *Polk Company News*, April 26, 2011.
10. Ken Smikle, "Volkswagen's New Marketing Chief: Black Consumers 'Important' to Sales Goal," *Target Market News*, October 19, 2011.
11. Ibid.
12. Diversity Affluence is a marketing communications and business development consultancy that specializes in delivering insights on Royaltons (affluent ethnic consumers).
13. Gary Lee, "Black Travelers Join the Club," *Washington Post*, September 3, 2006.

CHAPTER 5

Another Opportunity: Wellness Matters

All is not well within the Black community.

Obesity, high blood pressure, diabetes, heart disease and cancer are part of the major health challenges facing Black Americans. Add to that limited or inadequate health insurance coverage and restrictive access to preventive medical care, and the situation appears monumental.

Let's be honest. When it comes to wellness, things in the Black community don't look good. However, that frailty is exactly where the opportunity lies for marketers to become part of the community, to establish a presence, and to build trust. By helping the community confront and overcome these challenges, marketers can show a deep and full understanding of Black Americans, but they need to be creative with their approach.

This isn't going to be easy or quick.

For example, in a middle-class African-American neighborhood in Chicago, I counted between ten and twelve fast food restaurants within 10 consecutive blocks. Most were national chains with a few independents touting fried chicken, fried fish, hoagies, hamburgers with triple meat, super-sized fries and soft drinks, processed turkey, roast beef, corned beef and more. And to think, it's much worse in poorer neighborhoods. In these communities, there tends to be more independent fast food restaurants coupled with small grocers who will add cooked, fatty ground beef and processed cheese to a bag of corn chips upon request at an extra charge—an inner city version of chili cheese fries with corn chips instead of potatoes.

Add the high number of "food deserts" in urban communities (the lack of places to buy fresh produce and other healthy alternatives), to Black America's propensity for traditionally prepared "soul food" dishes, and you have the primary culprits for Black America's health challenges: eating the harmful, unhealthy foods and lack of exercise.

Clearly the African-American diet explains why obesity, hypertension/high blood pressure, heart disease, and diabetes continue their grip on the Black community at higher rates than other segments.

While many African Americans are well aware of their role in the perpetuation of these diseases, many also believe being Black is a primary cause for health challenges based on genetics, culture and just living Black in America:

- The underlying reality of some diseases to African Americans, like high blood pressure, for example, is that even if they do everything they are supposed to do to avoid or prevent this disease, they are still more susceptible to it because they're Black. As such, acceptance, apathy, and non-compliance on several levels rule the day because: "What's the point?"

- During separate focus group discussions with African-American patients who were diagnosed with hypertension and those who were diagnosed with diabetes, respondents young and old, male and female unanimously agreed that African Americans' health is affected not only by what they eat, but also because being Black "is the most stressful job in America." Author Touré writes about how bottled-up emotions related to pre- and post-racism have impacted the health of many in the Black community in five major ways, in his book, *Who's Afraid of Post-Blackness?*

- Almost exclusive to the working class: exposure to inadequate medical care.

- Commodities specifically marketed to or easily available in Black communities like junk food, substandard food, malt liquor, drugs, and others.

- Toxic substances and hazardous conditions (like asbestos or other sorts of harmful chemicals) used in housing projects or on blue-collar job sites.

- The impact of socially inflicted trauma (both mental and physical) stemming from racism experiences either directly or vicariously.

- Blacks who have extra human reasons why they need to win—to prove that they have been wrongly judged—find themselves working incredibly hard and straining the edge of their physical, mental and human capabilities.

- Faith and spirituality are interwoven in Black lifestyle and Black health. Many believe prayer is just as important as taking pills when treating any illness or disease.

- Where the general market may believe that the saying "Big Is Beautiful" is a myth or misconception, it is a fact that holds much truth and relevance in the African-American community. African-American men prefer their women "on the large" side (not obese). In fact 74 percent say they like a woman with "a little meat on her bones."[1] As such, this cultural preference for largeness has a major role in the high incidence of and difficulty in controlling obesity, high blood pressure, and diabetes among African Americans, especially women.

- Many African Americans believe physicians don't take them seriously, and therefore, tend to believe Black doctors have a better understanding of Black issues and African-American cultural issues.

    Findings from a qualitative study that our firm conducted in 2007 among Black and non-Black physicians with a sizable African-American patient base, revealed African-American doctors were unanimous in feeling that Black culture plays a role and even makes a difference in how African-American patients should be diagnosed and treated for particular diseases like high blood pressure and diabetes. Non-African-American doctors were not as convinced. They felt socioeconomic factors (e.g., poverty) were more causal, and African Americans just happened to be highly, even over-represented, below the poverty line.

African-American Doctors	Non-African-American Doctors
African Americans live differently with regard to their outlook on life, faith and their belief in home remedies:	Poverty is a primary determinant. Environmental situations also have much to do with hypertension as anything else:
"People in the Black community have a tendency to just live for the day."	"To me it's more the culture of poverty than African-American culture. It just so happens that African Americans are disproportionately represented below the poverty line.
"Many of my patients think that if they pray on their condition it will improve."	"I have a hard time grasping the cultural issues. Poor Whites eat just as much salt as poor Blacks."
"Home herbal remedies are replacing medication for many of my patients."	

Moreover, African-American doctors were very much in favor of developing materials specifically for African Americans and the use of media specifically targeting African Americans.

The Opportunities

Better health is just around the corner for this segment, but are marketers engaging this audience in a relevant way?

Paying attention to Black culture and learning about what's important and what's not, presents wide-open opportunities to extend a health message to this segment in a relevant and meaningful way. Here are a few insights to jump-start your thinking about engaging Black Americans around wellness:

- Many Black churches, beauty salons and barbershops are hubs for providing information and services to the Black community.

  Segmented Marketing Services, Inc., created "Healthy Living Every Day!" promotions that were executed over a four-year period involving multiple corporate partners and brands including Mazola, Mrs. Dash, St. Joseph low-dose aspirin, and insurance company, Aetna, to spread health information about combating these disparities.

  For Mrs. Dash, a "wet sample" (one of many sampling types), was used. Hot, low-salt spaghetti meals made by local Black chefs were delivered to Black churches and served in minority-owned restaurants. Luncheon speakers addressed the need to combat hypertension, a common problem in the Black community, with a low-salt diet. A custom *Urban Call*, headlined "Healthy Living Every Day!" accompanied the promotion and was distributed in churches, beauty salons and barbershops.

- Black sororities and fraternities represent thousands of "Good Samaritan" outlets for reaching the Black community nation-wide.

- There are hundreds of certified Black physical fitness trainers across the country that not only help many in the Black community transform from couch potatoes to active citizens, but also counsel them on diet and nutrition. Few companies have tapped into this group as a valuable resource.

- In 2012, nationally syndicated disc jockey, Tom Joyner will celebrate for the eleventh year in a row, the successful "Take a Loved One to the Doctor Day." Joyner does an all-out plea on his radio show to encourage African Americans to be more proactive about their health. On that day, *The Tom Joyner Morning Show* hosts and broadcasts with his *Morning Show* crew at "Doctor Day" health fair events in key markets. Activities include health screenings, HIV & AIDS rapid testing, immunizations, blood pressure exams, and more.

- Michelle Obama's war against obesity program encourages Americans to "get moving." Many companies take that message to the Black community via softball and basketball leagues, and to the Black church as mentioned earlier.

- Rallying the influencers to start weight loss groups and targeting walking clubs through many community outreach organizations is a great way to motivate Black Americans, given their affinity for group activities. Athletic shoe companies can become heroes, sponsoring these groups by providing exercise instruction and gear via contests.

Wellness in Black America also means overcoming its long history of the negative effects of traditional soul food meals. Although many African Americans can be flamboyant or meticulous in their style of dress, many are, at the same time, conservative about trying new foods and feel happy to be forever linked to a soul food diet.

A group of culinary historians, nutritionists and health experts from Oldways, a non-profit organization that promotes healthy eating based upon regional diet pyramids, has put together the Oldways African-Heritage Diet Pyramid. It is a new model for healthful eating designed specifically for African Americans and descendants of Africans everywhere. The pyramid draws from the culinary traditions of the American South, the Caribbean, South America, and Africa,. It shows familiar vegetables like okra and eggplant and fruits like papaya, as well as beans and meats. And unlike other food pyramids, it has a prominent layer devoted entirely to greens: collards, chard, kale and spinach—all foods of Africa and the diaspora regions of the Americas.[2] Although serving up this idea to 40- and 50-year-olds can be challenging, younger children who are learning about good nutrition in school are likely to grasp this idea and influence family members.

We saw evidence of this in a large-scale study that we conducted for a major food and beverage company in 2010. During focus group discussions about health and wellness among African-American parents, we learned that young children, acting as "food police" were positively impacting foods that went into the grocery cart, and onto the table at mealtime:

"Mommy, where are your vegetables?"

"Daddy your plate doesn't have enough colors on it!"

In the focus groups, parents explained that their children were learning about the food pyramid and getting nutritional information from Dora the Explorer—the animated cartoon character who embarks on a trip in every episode in order to find something or help somebody. As a result their children strongly influence them and other family members to eat better.

All may not be well within the Black community. However, the marketer who recognizes the opportunities that wellness issues present to build and strengthen a relationship with the Black community will discover healthy success.

The State of Black Health

- The American Heart Association suggests that 13 million African Americans over the age of 20 have diabetes, yet many more do not know that they do.

- A government study released in September 2010 shows that African Americans are nearly twice as likely to die from a heart-related disease than any other race.

- According to *Medline Plus Medical Encyclopedia*, this study shows that younger African Americans between the ages of 35 and 44 had almost twice the rate of heart attack, stroke or heart failure when compared with their White peers.

- According to the MUSC Heart and Vascular Center (Charleston, SC), African-American women in particular have nearly a 45% higher frequency of cardiovascular disease than White women. Another 41% of African-American women reported not knowing their risks.

- The American Heart Association suggests that African-American heredity and lifestyle factors have resulted in more than 77% of women and 63% of men over 20 years old developing a weight problem, which increases the risk of developing heart disease .

- The American Heart Association states that more than 40% of African Americans have hypertension.[3]

Notes

1. Essence/ AOL, "What Black Men Want: A Survey," www.essence.com/2005/06/28/what-black-men-want-a-survey, 2005.
2. Eliza Barclay, "How Soul Food Can Be Good for Your Health," NPR food blog, *The Salt*, November 10, 2011.
3. Robin Wood-Moen, "Genetic Factors of Heart Disease in African Americans," *www.Livestrong.com*.

Under the Radar:
Black Immigrants and Black Biracials

By J. P. James, Senior Partner, Engagement Planning, MEC

The populations of foreign-born, biracial Blacks and Afro Latinos are growing faster than the African-American segment. In most major cities, the percentage of the Black biracial, foreign-born and Afro-Latino population is as high as 25 percent.

The foreign-born Black segment is composed of Black-Caribbean, and Black-African immigrants. With a U.S. population nearing 4 million, African and Caribbean immigrants represent a unique segment of the Black population. The other segment is Black Biracials. The "one drop rule"—dictating that if people have even one drop of Black blood they are Black—is now debatable, but the mindset of someone who is biracial is unique in contrast to someone with two parents who are African Americans. Lastly, there is the Black- or Afro-Latino segment, a group within the Latino population.

According to the U.S. Census Bureau, approximately 1.7 million of the 38.8 million Latinos identified themselves as both Latino and of African descent, yet many experts believe this number to be closer to 3.9 million. More than 42 percent of all Latino respondents marked a box labeled "some other race" on the census form.

Black immigrants do not arrive in the United States as empty cultural containers waiting to be "Americanized." They come with perceptions, images, and values on issues of race, class and gender relations that are shaped in their home countries.

Most Black immigrants consider themselves Black (vs. African

American). Differences in culture, customs, language, and history keep these communities more insular. Chicago, for example, is generally (still) a segregated city, especially between Black and White residents. Blacks are primarily clustered on the south and west sides of the city, while Whites tend to live downtown, north, the far southwest side, and in suburbia.

Black immigrants tend to live in relatively concentrated areas on the north side of town. In Chicago, as well as other U.S. urban areas, Black immigrants are not generally part of the African-American mainstream. (*See* Black Immigrants vs. African Americans, *page 93*)

Similarly, they display multiple forms of identity related to the diverse racial, ethnic, and urban contexts in which they settle and work. They are proud of their heritage and maintain strong ties to their home countries. Not surprisingly, food has become one of the most popular connectors between life in the U.S. and their homeland.

During a 2010 ethnographic/shop-along study with U.S.-born African Americans from Chicago, Birmingham, Atlanta, and Washington, D.C., it was interesting that nearly half of the respondents were living in households (in each market) where the spouse or partner was a Black immigrant. Throughout the interview and shop-along, these U.S.-born respondents expressed interest in African and Caribbean seasonings and foods via connections with loved ones who are Black immigrants and those who are U.S. born first- and second-generation relatives of Black immigrants. These connections strongly influence what they buy and where they shop for particular food items.

Large grocers like Giant, Jewel-Osco, and Publix are paying attention to the growing number of African and Caribbean immigrants and are responding to their needs by stocking specialty food items in key areas such as the produce department, and in relevant sections of ethnic food aisles. (*See* Publix Wins with Caribbean Shoppers, *page 94*)

As with most immigrant groups who come to America, they are hard working and take pride in financially supporting loved ones left behind. Often, they are the sole source of income for their families living in their home countries.

African Immigrants

People could tell that I am an African by the sound of my name and accent. Whenever I am around people, they begin to ask questions about Africa. For example, someone asked me "do you walk around naked in Africa?" Another person asked me "do you live in huts at Africa?" This shows that these are the stereotypes people of other races have about Africa. They didn't know what the life in Africa looks like because they got these stereotypes from movies and Internet sources . . .

—Oluwasegun Akinola, blogger, *Stereotypes of Africa*

Taxi drivers—poor, voodoo-loving, and primitive—can also be included in his above list of common African-immigrant stereotypes. All these misperceptions, however, are quite contrary to their reality.

African immigrants tend to be better educated and have higher incomes than foreign-born Americans and U.S.-born African Americans. Thus, they are less likely to be in poverty or unemployed.[1] In fact, nearly one-third earn $50,000 or more by being employed in professional, technical, executive, managerial, and sales positions; or from owning and operating small successful family-based businesses.[2] Many African immigrants also consciously maintain the dress, language, and other aspects of their homelands to affirm their "otherness."

Although African immigrants do not share the legacy of slavery with their African-American counterparts, and because they come from countries in which Black people are the majority and control the government, these immigrants have had less personal experience with overt racism or segregation. However, as mentioned earlier, most are sensitive to negative stereotyping. Particularly, they are disturbed by the representation of themselves in the U.S. media and have expressed disappointment with both news and fictional work when it comes to their people, countries, and continent.

At the same time, the absence of negative history, combined with their quest for excellence in education translates to an unbridled confidence that is seen throughout the community, especially in their children and grandchildren.

Hanna is a second-generation Nigerian born in the United States. Her parents emigrated from Africa, settled in the U.S. and raised eight children, all of whom were born in the United States. Hanna is number six. At 27 she is the COO of a digital media company, and at this writing, is attending her first semester at Harvard to earn an MBA. Older brothers and sisters are high achievers too. They are lawyers, doctors, and executives who embrace the responsibility of performing well educationally and professionally.

Hanna has a diverse group of friends, but her close friends tend to be people of color—Black, Latino, and Middle Eastern. As imagined, Hanna has a busy life so it's important for her to be digitally connected to her friends and family, her work, and for school.

She's online 24/7 checking email, texting, reading current news and blogs—primarily from her Smartphone (bossip.com is one of her favorites), and is all over the net via her laptop, getting information for research papers and other assignments for school.

Caribbeans and Afro Latinos

Depending on who's doing the defining, Caribbean and Afro Latinos migrate from some of the same countries: Cuba, the Dominican Republican, and Puerto Rico. Noted countries of Caribbean migrants also include Haiti, Jamaica, Trinidad and Tobago, and Guyana, while countries of Afro-Latino migrants are Belize, Panama and Venezuela.

It's estimated that between 10 percent and 80 percent of Latinos, and 1.8 million Black Caribbeans hail from these countries. As the slave trade proliferated in the Americas from the 1500s through the 1800s, Europeans used Caribbean ports as a hub to transfer African slaves throughout North, Central, and South America, as part of the African Diaspora.

Some experts say Caribbean and Afro Latinos have as much or more in common with African Americans, as many regularly face discrimination and battle racism, both in the United States and in their native countries.

Countries of Origin for Caribbean and Afro-Latino migrants

Caribbean and Afro Latinos
Cuba
Dominican Republic
Puerto Rico

Caribbean Immigrants
Haiti
Jamaica
Trinidad & Tobago
Guyana

Afro Latinos
Belize
Panama
Venezuela

For dark-skinned Latinos in the United States, the American dream is often punctuated with dismaying experiences of trying to fit into a classification-oriented society. Black Latinos share a culture and language with White Latinos, but some say the race consciousness of America forces them to adopt an identity—as Black Americans—that is not really their own. If they forego the label, Afro Latinos say they still are treated as African Americans by most people and resented by some Blacks who they think are ashamed of their African heritage.

Alberto Padron addresses this on his blog:

"'I'm not Black, I'm Hispanic.' Black refers to race. Culture refers to ethnicity. These terms often get confused. The moment we start hyphenating the term Black, a clearer cultural picture begins to emerge. For example, when one encounters the term Black American (or African American) or Black Hispanic (or Afro Latino), one gains a better feel for the cultural orientation that is being referred to. Indeed, there is a relationship between color and culture, but when we make the two indistinguishable, confusion follows."

African Americans Are Not the Only Blacks

In the U.S., the African-American community largely monopolizes the term Black. The dialogue regarding race is either Black (African American) or White. Mr. Padron reminds us that Blacks from across the globe residing in America, who are not of African-American culture, are proud to claim their color (race) without apprehension that they will be mislabeled as U.S.-born African Americans.

Mr. Padron states that he looks like his Hispanic mom and even more so, his dark-skinned grandparents and cousins and embraces the term Black because it's part of who he is. Mr. Padron has fair-skinned Hispanic family members as well, resulting in a mix of races referred to as mulatto. He'd prefer that we embrace his color (Black) and combine it with his Hispanic culture and proudly declare what he and others from his culture are—Black Hispanic, Afro Latin, or mulatto.

According to a study by the State University of New York at Albany "How Race Counts for Hispanic Americans," Hispanics who define themselves as "Black" have lower incomes and are more likely to reside in segregated neighborhoods than those who identify themselves as "White" or "other." Most Black Hispanics, the study found, come from the Dominican Republic and Puerto Rico.

Caribbean immigrants have had different experiences of racial discrimination in the United States, depending on their racial background. Historically, White immigrants received better treatment by immigration authorities than their Black counterparts.

At the same time, many tend to be well educated, middle-class, and loyal consumers. Although their primary language is English, many Caribbean Americans also speak French, Spanish, Portuguese, or Creole.

A colleague of mine, Magda Guillaume, was born in Haiti and came to the United States when she was a pre-teen. For the purposes of this book, she was kind enough to share her experiences with me as a Black Caribbean immigrant.

Magda immigrated to America in the early 1970s. Being a Black immigrant in those days meant fitting into the African-American box of identity. There was a negative stigma about being a Black immigrant during this time, especially from Haiti. It was not until the late 1980s that you would see the burgeoning nationalistic pride and retro-acculturation that Black Caribbean immigrants have today. Before this time, Black immigrants were the invisible segment. And in marketer's eyes, they still are.

The Unique Trichtomous Identity

The approach to acculturation for the Hispanic segment also applies to Black Caribbean individuals. In her last book, *What's Black About It?* Pepper Miller mentions the dichotomous personality that African Americans have within their personal and private lives. Unique to Black immigrants is that they have a *trichotomous* identity—one with the general market, one with African Americans, and the last one with their identities from their cultures of origin.

The trichotomous identity explains why Magda states that she does not see her Black Haitian self in advertising and marketing communications. Because Black Caribbean immigrants are also an invisible segment, there are virtually no ads that speak to her as a Black Caribbean. Similar to African Americans, many Black Caribbeans zero in on advertising developed for them in search of authentic cultural connections. Thus being a Black immigrant from the Caribbean is more than alcohol (rum) or vacation spots. Marketers must get to know and understand the trichotomous identity of this segment.

The Identity Dilemma: Black, Hispanic, or White

There is a cultural divide that exists among Black Caribbean immigrants and African Americans—one where many of the African American filter insights do not apply. Marketers must get to know and understand the trichotomous identity of this segment. As the Latino population has grown in the United States, so has the number of Latinos of African descent. About 2 percent of the Hispanics in the 2000 Census identified themselves as "Black." That compares with close to half who said they were "White" and the 42.5 percent who described themselves as "some other race."

Since 1970, in addition to asking people to identify themselves by race, the U.S. census has asked people to indicate if they are either "Hispanic" or "non-Hispanic." "Hispanic" is considered an ethnicity, not a race; people of Hispanic origin can be of any race. Though Latinos who describe themselves as "Black" make up a very small percentage of the U.S.–Hispanic population, studies suggest their socioeconomic status is more akin to that of African Americans than other Latinos or Caucasian Americans.

Because Latin American culture fuses different cultures and races, many Latinos have unique experiences of being classified by others as White or Black, depending on the situation. Some say Latin Americans have a better sense of how important color is in the United States because they usually straddle the line between White and Black.

As mentioned earlier, although their primary language is English, many Caribbean Americans also speak French, Spanish, Portuguese or Creole. Thus, marketing campaigns targeting African Americans usually do not translate well to the Caribbean market. The large cultural celebrations of Caribbean Americans held around the country are ideal opportunities to show support for this growing consumer segment.

Black Immigrant Quick Facts[3]

Top five countries of origin for Caribbean immigrants

1. Cuba
2. Haiti
3. Jamaica
4. Trinidad & Tobago
5. Barbados

Geographic location of Black-Caribbean immigrants

Caribbean Americans are heavily concentrated on the East Coast and represent a significant portion of the Black population in these areas. The top five metro areas in which they reside are:

- New York City: 25.7% of the Black population
- Miami: 28.5% of the Black population
- Fort Lauderdale: 29.6% of the Black population
- Boston: 25.6% of the Black population
- Nassau-Suffolk, New York: 25.5% of the Black population

Neighborhood characteristics of Black-Caribbean immigrants

According to the U.S. Census Bureau, the average Caribbean resident lives in a neighborhood in which:

- Median income is $41,328 vs. $35,679 for the average Black resident.
- 49.8% of the residents are homeowners vs. 53.1% for the average Black resident.
- 20.3% of the residents are college educated vs. 17.5% for the average Black resident.

Geographic location of Black-African immigrants

Today, nearly 1.7 million people in the U.S. list their ancestry as sub-Saharan African, according to the U.S. Census Bureau.

- Ethiopians have settled primarily in California, Virginia, and Maryland.
- Ghanaians have settled primarily in New York, Texas, and Maryland.
- Nigerians have settled primarily in California, Texas, Maryland, and New York.

Black Biracials

"What are you?" is the question many young people freely (and unwisely) ask other young people of mixed race heritage. However, as those who are not of mixed race get older, and encounter a person who they think may be of "mixed race heritage," they learn not to ask the question, especially if you are Black. For many, the confusion of others over their racial identity is the biggest, and thorniest, issue.

The biracial sub-segment is a cultural enigma, and as a group, requires recognition and representation, but many in the segment are still searching to find or create a foundation of their own cultural infrastructure (i.e., many experience an inherent conflict of recognizing the other aspect of their "bi-ness"). Since the other aspects of their "bi-ness" could be either Caucasian, Latino, Asian, or something else, all of which have additional multi-dimensional cultural layers of origins, society has difficulty understanding their ethnic point of reference and therefore, tends to view Black biracials as nebulous and undefined. But Black biracials see themselves in the vanguard of this country's new and changing society as represented by our 44th President who has a distinct lineage of a Caucasian mother from Wichita, Kansas, and a Kenyan father from Kanyadhiang Village, Rachuonyo District, Kenya. All of which has encouraged new conversations and a 21st-century view on the Black biracial segment.

Being biracial isn't post race. It's not less race. It's another segment of race.

There were 784,764 U.S. residents who described their race as White *and* Black in the 2000 Census. The agency expects the number of people who choose multiple races overall to be significantly higher in the 2010 Census than the 2000 Census, when the government first allowed allow people to identify themselves by more than one race.

It's impossible to know how many of the 35 million people counted in 2000 as "Black alone" had a White parent. But it's clear that the decision to check one box—or more—on the census is often steeped in history, culture, pride, and mentality.

This also may represent a new twist on the "one drop" concept, which for centuries held that even one Black ancestor made a person Black. Forty years ago the prevailing notion was that biracial Americans didn't have a choice about their racial identity, that the wider society would view them as being African American. Now, this segment has an opportunity to proclaim all of its racial identities.

Mixed-race marriages have jumped 20 percent since 2000 to 4.5 million, or 8 percent of the total.[4] Society's acceptance of this group is seen through several movies and TV shows that feature mixed race coupling such as *Grey's Anatomy, The Practice,* and *The Game.* And many parents of biracial Black and White children are either encouraging their children to self identify based on their child's comfort level, or follow the traditional "one drop" practice: that is "as soon as your kids are old enough, they are Black people in America. They are not half of anything."

"I'm not going to put a label on it. I had to decide for myself and that's what she's going to have to decide—how she identifies herself in the world," says Oscar-winning actress, Halle Berry when asked, during an interview for *Ebony* magazine, about whether she considers her daughter, Nahla, whose father is French-Canadian Gabriel Aubry, Black or White? She continues, "And I think, largely, that will be based on how the world identifies her. That's how I identify myself. But I feel like she's Black. I'm Black and I'm her mother, and I believe in the one drop theory."[5]

Berry makes an interesting point. Regardless of how one feels, appearance may override any personal choice. Unlike mixed race individuals of other ethnicities, Afro-centric features (skin tone, hair texture, and facial appearance) are more dominant in Black biracial individuals.

Many Black biracials have also faced the all-too-familiar trappings of White racism against Blacks, and the ostracism by some African Americans who view biracials as less than full members of the Black community. In the May 5, 2010, post on stuffWhitepeopledoblogspot.com, guest blogger Brenda, who describes herself as a "half Black, half White young woman who is trying to discover what it means to be both and neither" writes:

"I feel under constant pressure to prove myself to White people, to prove that I'm Black. I study slavery, racial and social issues, problems in countries in Africa, all the things that (I assume) White people look for when determining if someone without typical Black characteristics can receive their 'Black' stamp of approval.

"Unfortunately, this way of thinking carries over into the Black community, and I find myself not being taken seriously when I tell other Black people how I feel. I've been laughed at and I've received the same confused expressions that I get from White people. . . . calling myself Black and being treated as a Black person are very different things."

Society generally thinks it is good for more people to consider themselves as multiracial instead of belonging to one race. At the same time, many also believe that broadened racial definitions can lead to greater racial fragmentation and could also negatively impact policies, funding, and initiatives intended for specific racial or ethnic groups. For example, the rise of the Black Diasporic populations means that this could fragment and decrease the size of the African-American population in the U.S. As discussed with Black Caribbean immigrants, the needs of African Americans and the Black sub segments are different. This may hurt historical and traditional African-American advocacy groups like the NAACP and National Urban League. Furthermore, some multiracial people expect marketers to address them in a culturally sensitive manner with the right "voice," i.e., one different from that used to address a single race.

We heard this request in 2009 from Black biracials during qualitative research that The Hunter-Miller Group conducted in several markets on behalf of the 2010 Census advertising campaign. Specifically, most biracial respondents across all markets expressed a preference for messages that reflected diversity, versus advertising that targeted African Americans.

Some companies and products target multiracial people directly or with appropriate cultural cues. New hair-care products, Miss Jessie's and Mixed Chicks, launched within the past few years, were specifically targeted to Black biracial women to help tame their naturally curly locks. The products attracted many African Americans who also choose to wear their hair naturally. Today, these multi-million dollar brands have inspired the launch of other "me too" brands and collectively, these products (for naturally kinky and curly hair) have become one of the new standards of hair care products within the $9 billion Black hair-care industry. At the same time, expanded racial classifications like Black biracials also present challenges with respect to policies, social programs and marketing. Therefore, distinct values and experiences must be understood to develop appropriate appeals.

As celebrating more than one race and heritage becomes more visible in the media, accepted and popular messages for 100 percent Blacks may not reach multiracial Blacks in the same way because their values, experiences, and racial identifications are different. Modifying or "diversifying" Black-targeted messages to incorporate the multiracial segment can risk alienating the initial target market—African Americans—while not reaching the broader audience of multiracial Blacks.

Marketing in the 21st century means having a global mindset. The same is true when marketing to Black consumers. Today's Black consumer is African, Caribbean, biracial, Latino as well as African American. The monolithic approach to this segment is obsolete.

Marketers, especially local marketers, should look at the population make up of the cities in which they do business. Instead of looking at only African-Americans, marketers should look at the population of the Black foreign-born as well as those who are Black and another race. This not only increases the size of the consumer potential but also allows for more effective marketing communications to the entire Diaspora. I would also recommend that the market research community assess ways to uniquely look at foreign-born Blacks and biracial Blacks in addition to African Americans in secondary research data. Marketing to Black consumers in the 21st century must take into account the entire Black Diaspora living in the United States.

Black Immigrants vs. African Americans
The Dichotomous vs. the Trichotomous Persona

In some African-American communities, relations with Black immigrants have at times been strained. In part, that comes from stereotypes and misperceptions that both sides have of one another.

Historically immigration probably has been one of the most difficult problems for the Black-American population of the United States. Many in the African-American community fail to understand the history of forced migration from African and Caribbean countries. The political, economic, and social crises that motivate Black immigrants to leave their countries to seek opportunities in America have eluded many U.S.–born African Americans. Thus, many tend to carry the perception that immigrant labor lessens job opportunities for lower-income African Americans.

At the same time, African and Caribbean immigrants do not always understand the historical legacy of racism in American society and the present day disparities that still challenge the lives of U.S.–born Blacks. These points explain why there is another layer of insight, a trichotomous persona, to Black immigrants who live in a world where they experience African Americans, Caucasians, and their own cultures.

———

Publix Wins with Caribbean Shoppers

By Matlock Advertising and Public Relations

Background/The Opportunity

Publix Super Markets proudly boasts about being "the largest and fastest-growing employee-owned supermarket chain in the United States" and explains that its success is attributed to making sure its customers have an enjoyable shopping experience.

Within Publix's home state of Florida, the West-Indian (Afro-Caribbean) population has continued to grow and become influential within African American and other segments. Given that cities like Miami and Fort Lauderdale have combined West-Indian populations of over 600,000, Publix sought to understand the unique needs, wants, concerns and cultural differences inherent within this market segment so that it could target communications directly to them.

Through Relevant Research We Took a Closer Look at the Target

Matlock identified West-Indian women in Miami and Fort Lauderdale as primary shoppers of their households for conducting focus group and ethnographic research. A series of videotaped ethnographies and shop-alongs that followed them through their shopping and cooking experiences were conducted. Each ethnography captured comments, cultural nuances, and cooking methods from which we developed a comprehensive understanding of Publix's West-Indian customer.

Observations and implications gleaned from the research were used to enhance Publix's strategies in marketing, product offerings, recruitment and operations within West-Indian neighborhoods.

The Publix Caribbean Shopper Approach

Objectives	The Plan
Build relationships with target	• Create Independence Day events among key West-Indian countries, i.e., Jamaica, Barbados, Bahamas, Trinidad/Tobago. • Create supporting celebration print and radio campaigns
Increase awareness of relevant product offerings	• Sponsor West Indian–targeted radio stations in South Florida. • Sponsor/create food related events/festivals such as the Publix Jerk Festival (Title Sponsor).
Encourage transactions of relevant products	• Developed print campaign in targeted West-Indian print media. • Created the Caribbean Fest direct mail and in-store POP program.
Support internal efforts	• West Indian Action Guide, a proprietary binder for Publix that details who West-Indian shoppers are, the foods they like, and their social/celebratory activities. • Used *Apron's Simple Meals*, a Publix program where in-store kiosks feature cooking demonstrations and videos on preparing simple, healthy meals quickly, to feature West-Indian dishes. • Provided product recommendations of food items that should be stocked to meet West-Indian shopper needs.

Results: Miami Division

Sales increased in top 10 West-Indian stores

Key Performance Indicators: During the promotional period, sales and store traffic showed the following results:

- Increase in total store sales: 1.6%

- Increase in customer counts: 0.6%

- Increase in unit sales: 2.0%

Increased Brand Awareness

- Positioned Publix Super Markets as the authority on food
- Established "Food as History" campaign
- Established as a company that respects the African-American experience
- Educated target on initiatives for economic empowerment

Building Relationships

- Improved community relationships
- Developed minority purchasing program
- Negotiated community/grassroots sponsorships
- Created "Publix Minutes"
- Black History Month television

Improve Customer Transactions

- Identified factors that addressed initial declines in customer count; addressed them and increased customer visits and sales
- Used radio to reinforce invitation to purchase
- Focused print on high volume items
- Developed in-store customization and merchandising

Notes

1. Mary Mederios Kent, "Immigration and America's Black Population," *Population Bulletin,* December 2007.
2. Ibid.
3. Mintel Market Research, 2009.
4. Haya E. Nassar, "Multiracial No Longer Boxed In by the Census," *USA Today,* March 15, 2010.
5. Amy DuBois Barnett, "On the Very Solid, Fantastically Full Life of Halle Berry, *Ebony,* March 2011.

CHAPTER 7

Under the Radar:
The Black LGBT Community
By Reginald Osborne, Senior Vice President, Arnold Worldwide

The question "Am I Black?" or "Am I gay?" emphasizes the dilemma that is an internal struggle for many LGBT African Americans. It is similar to having to choose between being Black and American. The reality is that we are fluid and multidimensional. We can be both, just as Black LGBT members who are serving in the armed forces are American, Black, and LGBT.

The Challenge to Be Black, Gay, and Authentic

Many in the African-American focus group snickered or rolled their eyes at Boris after he revealed that he was gay. But Boris pressed on, not flinching or losing his train of thought. He's been here before. He ended his statement—the answer to the moderator's question—by saying that his most important personal value is "to be authentic."

To be authentic is really challenging for Black LGBTs. According to "Life Outside the Box," a study conducted by New American Dimensions, a Los Angeles-based market research firm that specializes in multicultural and LGBT segments. The study explores the lives of gay and lesbian African Americans and reports:

The African-American community has a clear, unwavering code against homosexuality, rooted in the church. Coming out, many gay African-American males face negative responses from all sides—friends, family, the church, and their community at large.

They no longer feel welcomed at home, social events, community hangouts, clubs, basketball courts, or in the church, and many feel a keen sense of isolation. Reactions are not as severe for African-American lesbians. They report losing African-American friends and church friends, especially female friends, but gaining some male ones.[1]

As America continues to struggle with race relations, for many Blacks, the addition of being gay, adds another level of complexity. One would think there would be much more cohesion within the LGBT community given that, as a whole, they continue to be ostracized by many in the mainstream. But the reality is, there is still a lot of segregation within the LGBT community.

Essentially, many in the Black gay/lesbian community and in other gay communities of color, do not feel a part of their White gay counterpart's projects, programs, and events. The evidence is that in most major cities, the bars and clubs are segregated. There are bars that cater to White, Black, and Hispanic LGBT. In major cities throughout the country, there is usually a Pride celebration that is mainly for Whites, and then there is a Black Gay Pride Celebration.

Marketing to the LGBT community is primarily focused on gay men and lesbians are treated as a non-entity. This is certainly true within the Black LGBT community. However, Black lesbians should not be overlooked because they are an important consumer segment. They are more likely to be partnered with children, and own a home.

Recently, I embarked on a nine-day cruise to the Mediterranean with a group of 28 LGBT members. To my surprise about half of the group was comprised of lesbians, and most of them were partnered. During the cruise I became better acquainted with a few of the couples. Most of them were professionals, educated and affluent.

One woman had just completed her graduate degree, was an entrepreneur and lived in a two-bedroom penthouse with her partner in Manhattan. Another woman was partnered with a woman who was a physician. They were well dressed with designer shoes, bags, and jewelry. Not to mention that we were all traveling on Norwegian—one of the higher-end cruise lines.

With some exceptions, many LGBT adjust by dating within their own ethnic group. In fact, some respondents from the "Life Outside the Box Study" say dating someone of your own ethnicity reduces problems in the relationship. African-American men say that other African-American men can also relate to the challenges of being African American in America.

The daily experience for the Black LGBTs also presents pressures in the workplace.[2] A survey commissioned by the Human Rights Campaign (HRC) revealed that out of 761 LGBT participants, only 25 percent of African Americans reveal their status on the job.[3] Additionally, unlike mainstream LGBTs who have a community that is a defined geographic location with retail stores, restaurants, and bars, Black LGBTs are more likely to gather at various locations. As a result of these and other related circumstances and behaviors, many Black LGBTs have adopted a "taking care of our own" approach by making an investment to satisfy their needs, and those of others like them who are tired of being shut out. Many Black LGBTs who remain closeted find the internet and social networking sites appealing as a way to stay connected to the community. Two examples of popular sites are:

- **Rod 2.0** is a leading weblog and webzine for urban gay men. It features information on pop culture, politics, Black gay culture, fashion, books, activism, HIV, AIDS, sports, media, television and more.

- Most popular for Black lesbians is the website for the **United Lesbians of African Heritage,** uloah.com. It draws thousands of Black women daily who are attracted to the organization's mission to promote visibility and unity among lesbians of African descent, thereby increasing wellness, acceptance and understanding in their lives.

Other visible signs that the Black LGBT community is thriving and creating opportunities to stay connected with and empower each other are the over 30 Black Pride festivals that occur in large and small cities throughout the United States and in Canada.

Many Black Pride festivals begin during the week and conclude on the weekend. In addition to hosting multiple parties, some of the festivals feature empowerment seminars, film screenings, book signings, and live entertainment. The largest Black Pride events are in Washington, D.C., and Atlanta, Georgia, and they attract well over 35,000 to 100,000 attendees.[4] Despite the impressive attendance numbers, organizers of the events contend that it is still difficult to attract major advertisers and corporate sponsors. It's shocking and disturbing to see marketers skip the opportunity to invest in these Black pride events and fund "other" Pride events that have smaller audiences.

Media for Black LGBTs

The proliferation of media content about the lives of Black LGBTs is another example of the self-contained economic success in the Black LGBT community.

For example, the late E. Lynn Harris became a successful author by telling stories centered on Black gay characters. He would go to Black LGBT events from city to city and sell his books from the trunk of his car. Initially his audience was primarily Black gay men but expanded to include Black women. Lynn is credited with spawning a cottage industry of Black gay romance novels and paved the way for other novelists like James Earl Hardy and his series of novels—B-Boy Blues.

Patrik-Ian Polk created and directed an independent film called *Punks* that became an instant hit with the Black LGBT community. Patrik used the premise of *Punks* to create *Noah's Arc*, which is the first scripted show on Logo, the LGBT cable channel. *Noah's Arc* was ground-breaking in that it was also the first "dramedy" to focus on the lives of four African-American gay men. And after Logo canceled the series after just two seasons, Patrik brought closure to the series by creating and producing the movie *Noah's Arc: Jumping the Broom*. Patrik's success paved the way for other independent LGBT films and filmmakers like Maurice Jamal who wrote and directed two successful independent LGBT movies *Ski Trip* and *Dirty Laundry.*

Lee Daniels is a rarity in Hollywood. He is a Black filmmaker with mainstream success—*Monster's Ball* and *Precious*—and he is openly gay. I can't help but think that his sexuality played a role in developing the lesbian couple in the movie *Precious.* When you begin to see LGBT characters represented in an authentic and proud manner in Black mainstream movies, it helps to create more dialogue, which in turn will lessen the homophobia.

The Future: A New Outlook

Black LGBTs are at a tipping point and on the verge of moving from the wings to center stage. According to a 2009 *Black Enterprise* article, the corporate behavior and response toward lesbian, gay, bisexual, and transgender professionals is changing. More Black LGBT professionals are being accepted, according to a recent survey from the Corporate Equality Index of 2010. Professional companies are increasing their recruitment activities and events to attract the LGBT Community.

A recent study from Out & Equal Workplace Advocates indicates more corporate activities are planned in the Black LGBT communities to attract a more diversified and qualified group of talented professionals. The outcome from this effort would deliver on the following goals:

- They can work more comfortably in the workplace.
- Believe there is a stronger embrace for more diversity.
- Believe there is some achievement in terms of workplace acceptance for all sexual orientations and gender identities.

Although the "down low" is still a big deal in the Black LGBT community, the changing attitudes and (slow) growing acceptance of the gay community discussed above has encouraged many to abandon their clandestine behavior and step boldly and fearlessly out of the closet.

Within the last couple of years, LGBT Black public figures, such as Don Lemon, a reporter for CNN, have come out of the closet. Don had been out to co-workers, family and friends but made the decision to let the world know he was gay while struggling to write a book on transparency. He recently wrote an article published in *Essence* magazine expressing his concerns about rejection from Black women given the homophobia in the Black community.

During the same week that Don Lemon came out, Will Sheridan, a former power forward for Villanova who is African American also came out. Wanda Sykes, an African-American comedian came out of the closet and has been a big supporter of gay marriage. And in Worcester, Massachusetts, the local NAACP elected an openly gay man, Ravi Perry, to serve as president of its chapter.

I often flip through the advertising pages of national and local gay publications and rarely will I see an advertisement for a product or service that speaks to me as a Black gay man. And I asked myself, why not? After all, I am a consumer of high-end skin-care products, premium vodka, luxury cars and vacations, and there are thousands like me. When it comes to LGBT marketing, the assumption is that we all are basically the same, having the same needs and wants. Therefore, this premise is partially the reason why the LGBT community and gay people of color are not on the radar screen of marketers as a viable niche market. Is it intentional oversight? Or is it that the decision makers sitting at the gay marketing table are not LGBT people of color, which results in strategies and campaigns that exclude rather than welcome.

Marketing to the LGBT community is still relatively new and has been in practice only within the last 15 years. I stopped in my tracks when I saw two Black men as a gay couple in a Wells Fargo ad. Not only gay, but also Black. Not only Black, but also gay. I felt an immediate appreciation of the brand. It felt good to see a company step toward the Black gay community to let us know that we matter and are valued.

Reginald Osborne is SVP/Director of Multicultural Marketing at Arnold Worldwide.

Additional Resources

- GBMNews
- Living Out Loud with Darian
- NoMoreDownLowTV.com

There are also specific Facebook pages:

- Adodi General
- Brothers Helping Brothers OUT
- Men4Men

Advertisers who have featured LGBT people of color:

- Wells Fargo
- Amtrak

Notes

1. David R. Morse, "Life Outside the Box: An Exploration of the Lives of Gay and Lesbian African Americans," ReachingBlackConsumers.com, September 2011.
2. "The Black LGBT Community: A New Outlook," *Market Snapshot,* January 26, 2011.
3. H.L. Davis, "The Black Gay Dollar: Ignored and Overlooked," www.dissidentvoice.org, January 27, 2006.

Black LGBTs
Truths, Insights, and Opportunities

By Howard Buford, President/CEO, Prime Access Inc.

The Dodge

Black gays and lesbians, or more broadly Black LGBTs, are too small of a group to target. The volume at stake is limited. Besides, we already reach them, as well as the rest of the LGBT market, when we reach the general market.

The Truth

Black LGBTs identify first as being Black, but also maintain many of the sensibilities of the overall LGBT experience. This makes them a unique target that exists alongside the LGBT and the African-American communities, giving rise to a desire and need to be acknowledged and addressed directly for who they are and how they live their lives.

The Insight

These consumers feel frustration and exclusion from the White gay and lesbian community as well as the larger African-American community, which can be disapproving and in denial of their existence. Speak to the unique identity of Black gays and lesbians, recognizing that they are particularly sensitive to being clumped in with the gay and lesbian community as a whole or with the Black community as a whole without direct portrayals or recognition of who they are, their life experience, and their sensibilities and concerns.

Separately, the larger LGBT community is often at the forefront of lifestyle trends and its members are innovators and taste makers for the general population. Many of the fashion designers and lifestyle and entertainment experts are members of the LGBT community and are in positions to influence the trends and brand choices of the larger marketplace. This is particularly true of popular culture such as fashion and entertainment where LGBTs are viewed as innovators and arbiters of taste, high-image brands such as spirits and luxury goods, and electronics where they are early adopters.

The Opportunity

Black gays and lesbians often serve as innovators and role models for this larger LGBT community. (Think of RuPaul on the Logo Network.) Additionally, Black gays and lesbians often serve as the innovators and trendsetters for the African-American community as well, that is a major arbiter of "cool" for the nation. Black LGBTs serve as the nexus for igniting brands into both these audiences, who in turn, carry them to the general population.

———

Howard Buford is the president/CEO of Prime Access Inc., a multicultural advertising agency, which creates traditional and digital marketing communications targeting African-American, Hispanic and gay consumers.

CHAPTER 8

Under the Radar:
Black Men

Black Men: At the Center of Cool, Swagger, Mass Influence . . . and Under the Radar

The Society Pages recently ran a provocative post in its Citings and Sightings blog: *understanding the difficulties of young black males*. The writer, Amelia, reiterated stories about young Black men that we've all heard and, in a strange way, tend to accept:

> They are overrepresented in the ranks of the unemployed and the incarcerated, and underrepresented as college students, as live-in husbands, and as fathers raising children. . . . Perhaps most important, young Black men are among the most misunderstood people in America.[1]

Mass media tend to emphasize disadvantaged Black males—gangsta rap, being "down with the homies"—and marginalize the good things about them.

There is a subgroup of young Black men (aged 18 to 30) who are the epitome of cool, professional and focused. They have "swag" or "swagger" which is contagious, as these young Black men have a growing presence and influence in the Black community.

This new group is changing the way we see, interact and most importantly connect with Black men in media.

Black men are garnering a lot of attention not only for their fashion, music and cultural preferences but also for how they conduct themselves.

The distance between the image being presented in the media and the reality of what is being seen in the community is growing. This is a change that marketers need to be aware of and address in their messaging.

The reality is that demographically, Black men tend to be younger (average age 29 vs. 35 for White), and as a segment, have been growing three times the rate of the White males. Although educational attainment fluctuates, more young Black men today are recognizing and embracing education as a means for overcoming societal barriers and advancing themselves.

Over the past 16 years, Black men have improved their secondary education graduation rate from 28 percent to 36 percent.[2] According to government figures, more than twice as many young Black men are now enrolled in college than are imprisoned.[3]

They Are Getting Involved

Increasingly, Black men are seeking and assuming significant roles in business, politics, sports entertainment and other areas. The Black America Study identifies one of its eleven segments as "Black Onliners."

This segment includes a majority of Black men who are 97 percent online, educated, and are moderate-income earners. Men within this segment are also networking with other professional Black men, have a majority of Black friends, and respond favorably to targeted Black advertising.

Just because the media aren't paying attention doesn't mean this shift isn't being noticed. Take the story of Clayton and LaNise Ollarvia's wedding:

The wedding was wonderful, like something out of a romantic movie. She was the classic, beautiful bride and he was the handsome groom. There were the proud and tearful parents, lively guests, fabulous music and food and the picture-perfect bridal party.

And as beautiful as the bride was, I found my attention being drawn to the constant conversations taking place from every corner of the wedding reception about Clayton's groomsmen. At the tables, at the bar, even in the restroom, guests were buzzing about the groomsmen—the charm, intelligence and wit of these young men was making a huge impression. The groomsmen's behavior sparked conversations and questions as to why there were not more positive stories and images of Black men in the media.

Importantly, many surmised—unaided by this researcher—that the groomsmen's behavior was not uncommon in the Black community. This was the story not being told.

The concern about the lack of positive African-American images in the media is picking up momentum. CNN anchor Soledad O'Brien, in a presentation to predominately African-American Kellogg graduate students and alumni at Northwestern University's Evanston, Illinois, campus, underscored the concern voiced by Ollarvia's wedding guests about the lack of positive African-American images in the media.

Using an exaggerated example to make a point about the need for balancing positive images of ethnic consumers in the media, O'Brien explained that whereas there are hundreds of stories about Whites in the media, "there are only 5 about Blacks, 3 about Latinos, 1 about Asians, and 0 for Native Americans." O'Brien reiterated what we have often heard: these group are protective about their image and have strong opinions about how they want America to perceive them. The head nods and whispers of agreement from my fellow audience members not only encouraged O'Brien, but also demonstrated how far the media has not come. (Quite honestly, it was the undeniable zero for Native Americans that made O'Brien's exaggerated example a bleak reality.)

The Mainstream Media Doesn't Get It

Why is it so hard to believe that Black men have positive dreams and stories? Why is the idea of positive Black men such a foreign concept to mainstream media? There is no easy or absolute answer.

The first part of the answer has to do with an unfamiliarity with the Black community by portions of the White population. Add to that the lack of a real conversation about race, the lingering effects of slavery and Jim Crow, the portrayals of Blacks in media, and it becomes easier to see how it could be more acceptable to view Black men in a negative light. Joblessness, crime, lack of education, and absentee fathers are more accepted images of Black men because they are closer to the stereotypical views many have grown up with. Thus, Black men tend to be one of, if not the most, vilified segments in the media—but not within the Black community.

Black America itself has struggled at times with these challenges. It isn't immune. The Black community recognizes that there is another side that is seldom told or shared outside of the community.

On the fireplace mantle in the home of Mary Miller sits the picture of Andrew Jackson. Not the seventh President of the United States, but grandfather to the Miller children, Mary, Ron, Shirley, and Beverly. Grandpa Jackson's picture is the largest picture on the mantle, and appropriately so. A man of small stature, he was larger than life. He was a teacher, preacher, single parent, and inventor of two patented items: eyeglasses for cockfights, and a device to keep tractors in a straight line for plowing fields. Born in the 19th century, some years after Emancipation, Grandpa Jackson was a stern disciplinarian who gave and demanded respect. He lived proudly and fearlessly in the Jim Crow south—emphasis on living fearlessly and Jim Crow south.

The stories that stood out about Grandpa Jackson were not his inventions, *per se,* but how he lived and how he was an example for the community. It was not uncommon for Grandpa Jackson to direct White delivery and service people to the back door to mirror Blacks who were forced to do the same in his lifetime. It was that "stand up" behavior that tipped the scale and made Grandpa Jackson a "hellava" man.

Like Grandpa Jackson's, there are thousands of stories that cycle through the Black community about good Black men. Only a few make it to the mainstream, but not enough to break the misperceptions and stereotypes.

What About These Men?

Ever heard of Phil Jackson? No, not the Lakers Coach, but the head of The Black Star Project. He founded the Chicago based organization in 1996, and has since been relentless about eliminating the racial academic achievement gap between mainstream and Black and Latino students locally and nationally.

What about Tim King, founder and CEO of Urban Prep Academies, a non-profit organization operating a network of public college-prep boys' schools in Chicago (usually African American) including the nation's first all-male charter high school.

John Hunter is the former owner/director of the Austin Academy of Fine Arts, a classical music school that he moved from Chicago to Greenville, South Carolina. Today it continues to primarily serve the Black community. Hunter's high standards for quality classical music education inspired current owner Tim Arnold and his students to seek and embrace excellence in everything they do, from attending master classes taught by prominent classical musicians, to wearing formal dress for recitals.

The guys in our neighborhoods are great fathers, terrific husbands, and stellar businessmen like attorney Greg Wilson, Al Grimes, Ronald Miller, Rev. Otis Moss III, Willie Calhoun, Brad Sanders, Brandon Miller, Andrew Honeywood, Alvin Alassane Jackson, Ananiais Grainger, Will Abernathy, Mike Ferguson, Curtis R. Monday, Craig Gilmor and Adam Farmer—good men representing different walks of life, yet their goodness is overshadowed by the imbalance of mainstream stories and the dreadful news clips about the Black man's plight that tend to stereotype all Black men.

Black men are also a positive presence in the Black community:

- **Real Men Charities** is the corporate entity behind the Real Men Cook brand, and since 1990, the nationally recognized Father's Day event has seen hundreds of men participating each and every year. The event attracts thousands in over 15 cities who enjoy sampling their favorite dishes that the men have volunteered to prepare. Numerous men have attached themselves to the summer day of fun in the sun since the beginning, and they continue to involve themselves and their entire families to share in this amazing love fest of men motivating and inspiring other men.[4]

- **Real Fathers, Real Men:** For the past 10 years, syndicated radio host Tom Joyner presents real, positive, authentic stories about Black fathers. He honors one every week during a special segment on his popular and syndicated Tom Joyner Morning Show, which runs daily in over 150 markets.

- **100 Black Men of America:** Dating its beginnings back to 1963, this group has been mentoring and creating programs designed to improve conditions in the Black community. Formally named 100 Black Men of America in 1986, with 116 chapters and over 10,000 members, it has been a positive presence in the Black community for decades.

- **Churches, Civil Rights organizations, Fraternities,** and others have always had a strong presence in the Black community, addressing a variety of issues and conditions. It was the Alpha Phi Alpha fraternity that led the funding and design for the Martin Luther King Jr. monument. Let's not forget the countless fathers, barbers, doctors, lawyers, teachers, coaches and others who have always been present in the Black community.

Positive examples abound. The smart marketer recognizes this and uses it to build stronger communications with the Black community. When done properly the results can be a marketer's dream.

Burrell Communications skipped the clichéd route of featuring a mom loading or unloading clothes in a washer in its TV commercial for P&G's Tide with Downy. Instead we see a Black father lovingly wrapping his young son in a soft fluffy towel after the child's bath. Not only did the commercial communicate Tide with Downy's "soft" benefits, it also showcased a Black man in a positive role. This scenario is an obvious learning extension from the hugely successful 2006 Tide with Downy TV commercial where Burrell featured a Black child and his father, clad in white t-shirts, napping together on crisp white sheets. As a result of Tide telling a new story about Black men as caring caretakers (primarily to Black women, I might add), reactions from the Black community were astonishing and continue to deliver successful ROI for the Tide brand.

It also demonstrates the power of bringing Black men and positive stories about them into the forefront of ad campaigns, communications, events, and cause- related marketing.

Hello, America

Not all Black fathers are dead-beat dads. In fact, Black men are taking more responsibility for their families. Two-parent families increased at nearly double the U.S. rate from the last census. And, according to *Essence* magazine's October 2009 Survey on Black Men in the Age of Obama, 44 percent of the men say they have seen more Black men spending time with their children.[8]

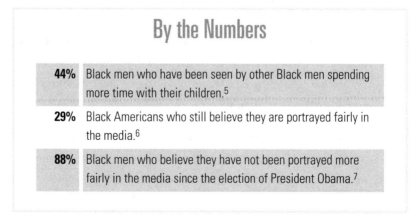

By the Numbers

44% Black men who have been seen by other Black men spending more time with their children.[5]

29% Black Americans who still believe they are portrayed fairly in the media.[6]

88% Black men who believe they have not been portrayed more fairly in the media since the election of President Obama.[7]

To understand and leverage the "Under-the-radar" phenomenon, marketers must appreciate that:

Good men and good fathers are heroes in any community. But good Black men and great Black fathers are superheroes in the Black community; their images are arresting, memorable, meaningful, motivational and extremely effective in engaging the Black community.

Marketers seeking to realize more success from the Black community need to look more deeply at the image and role of Black men in their marketing and advertising. The images don't have to be unrealistic but they can no longer be shallow either. It's time to take a deep look at Black men, and who they really are. (*See* Know Who You Are Really Talking To, *page 139*)

Notes

1. Amelia, "Understanding the Difficulties of Young Black Males, *The Society Pages, Citings and Sightings,* January 29, 2009.
2. "Black Student College Graduation Rates Inch Higher but a Large Racial Gap Persists," *The Journal of Blacks in Higher Education,* 2007.
3. Blackdemographics.com.
4. TruthBTold News Service/MG Media, June 17, 2011; www.realmencook.com.
5. Essence, Survey of Black Men, 2009.
6. Yankelovich and Associates / Radio One, Black America Today Study, 2008.
7. Essence, Survey of Black Men, 2009.
8. "Black Men in the Age of Obama," *www.essence.com,* October 2009; "Essence.com Survey of Black Men Finds Them More Optimistic in Obama Era," Target Market News, October 13, 2009.

Flip the Script and Tell the Story That's Rarely Told

The best insights lie in the deepest recesses. And the most original concepts are yet to be unearthed due to the fear of the unknown.
—Craig Brimm, founding blogger, KissMyBlackAds.blogspot.com

The benefit of showcasing positive Black men is garnering attention from the Black community. A good Black man is the unequivocal aspirational super hero in the Black community. Present as many positive images of him to the Black community (and the world) as possible. Show him in the manner that most want others to see him: confident, strong, cool, and caring.

Missed Opportunities: Current mainstream images are short on:

- Black men positively interacting with one another (rather than as adversaries)
- Generations of Black men working together
- Generations of Black men loving Black women
- Successful working Black men who are:
  - Executives/professionals
  - Involved with technology/science/engineering
  - Entrepreneurs
  - Everyday working men (i.e., policemen, firemen, construction workers)
  - Artists

———

CHAPTER 9

Under the Radar:
Black Baby Boomers

"You're old school." A simple comment made by a younger person as a rebuttal to an older person's point of view at a gathering at a mutual friend's home.

Nothing out of place for the lively and interesting group discussion that covered the variety of trending topics, except how it managed to divide the once cohesive group by age. It isn't the comment that divided the group; the real issue is the implied meaning that because of the person's age he or she doesn't matter or is no longer relevant. That's the problem.

And it is a problem many marketers share—they seem to think Black Baby Boomers don't matter or are not relevant.

Black Baby Boomers are old school.

"Old school" can reference a genre, a period of time, methods, and in the case of the comment made by the young person at the gathering, a group of people and a mindset. More often than not, especially in the Black community, many use this term for the latter description to imply being old fashioned and outdated. It comes from the generational differences between pre- and post-Civil Rights mindsets that create a wedge between older and younger African Americans. Born between 1946 and 1964, Black Baby Boomers have made educational, employment, and socio-economic gains since the Civil Rights Era. They represent the highest income segment of all African-American consumer groups.

They're investing, traveling internationally, volunteering, and mentoring; Black Boomers are philanthropic.

However, this group is often overlooked as a significant target because the differences between it and general-market Boomers are misunderstood.

Consciously or subconsciously Black Boomers tend to connect the dots, measuring their lives between today and the Civil Rights Era. While they live in the present, they have an acute understanding of the history and struggles of their community. They tend to measure themselves by how far they have advanced in relation to their parents and older relatives. They feel more accepted than their parents, but they do not necessarily link themselves with others in their Boomer generation. They view themselves as walking in two distinctly different worlds: the world where they work and live, and the world of African Americans' struggle for equality.

It is that division, in part, that contributes to them being ignored by marketers, but the main reason is tied back to the comment of the young person—they are old school. People are always looking for something new and advanced, the latest trend, and the coolest new thing. Marketers are no different. When it comes to trying to increase their market presence, Millennials are the latest, coolest, new thing for marketers.

There is a natural inclination to gravitate towards the "new" and "different" and away from the old and the familiar. While there is nothing wrong with that, marketers should consider that the Black Boomer market has gone largely untapped.

How did the Black Boomers go unnoticed? Marketers mistakenly thought Black Boomers were part of their overall outreach to Boomers. All boomers are not the same.

Black Boomers embrace Black pride and have high levels of self-esteem. They are not victims. In fact, they share more similarities with GenXers than their elders. They revel in the accomplishments and contributions of African Americans since the Civil Rights Era, but, as mentioned earlier, believe "the struggle" for racial equality is ongoing.

Moreover, they believe the struggle has been heightened (and not lessened per mainstream Boomers) by the election of Barack Obama as the first Black President of the United States.

This mindset has drawn many closer to Black culture, and many have become more concerned about the welfare of the Black community. The NAACP has seen increased membership primarily from this older segment that continues to find relevance in the organization compared with the younger generation.

It's Black Boomers who are wholly invested in Black media. They use it to remain connected to the Black community. Black talk radio, for example WVON (1690 AM) in Chicago and *The Power of African-American Talk* on Sirius XM Satellite Radio, have become richly important vehicles in the Black community, but particularly for Boomers. They tune in and call in often to participate in serious discussions with popular syndicated hosts including Rev. Al Sharpton, Warren Ballentine, Bev Smith, and Tavis Smiley, about issues considered critical by the Black community. It isn't only the Black talk radio format that has a connection with Boomers. Boomer radio hosts Tom Joyner, Steve Harvey, Doug Banks, and Michael Basiden have proven time and again that they have the ability to influence and motivate their listeners to take up a cause or action.

If marketers want to reach Black Boomers, then they need to tune into Black radio and other Black media.

Black Boomers are also socially conscious; often their support of a company or brand partially depends on that company's respect for their traditions and culture. They may not march or picket, but they are often willing to protest with their wallets. Black Boomers recognize the spending power they represent and are beginning to mobilize to better leverage that power.

John and Maggie Anderson of Oak Park, Illinois, made headlines in December 2008 when they pledged to help jump-start the economy by exclusively supporting Black-owned businesses for an entire year beginning January 1, 2009. With guest appearances on CNN and Fox News, and articles about their buy-Black proposition in local and national print and online media including *The Chicago Sun Times, Advertising Age*'s The Big Tent, and *The Huffington Post,* the Anderson's put their Empowerment Experiment on the map in a big way. Two years later, the Andersons have a book deal and an expanded vision to "trigger a smart movement where Americans of all backgrounds will unite to support quality minority businesses and ensure that the American Dream truly applies to all."[1]

Boomers Give Back

The practice of "giving back" is a big deal in the Black community. The traditional practice of tithing—giving back to God—among African-American Christians continues to be more consistent among Black Boomers than all other segments. According to bet.com, a recent study, "Cultures of Giving: Energizing and Expanding Philanthropy by and for Communities of Color" commissioned by the W.K. Kellogg Foundation, with major funding by the Rockefeller Philanthropy Advisors, reports that Blacks are actually 25 percent more likely than Whites to donate money. Further, many are expanding their giving to organizations outside of the church, especially to those that support Black community interests. Consider the giving practices of Lauryn and Anita.

Lauryn, a bank executive, tithes regularly at her church, and gives to other organizations that she feels are "relevant" to her giving sensibility. She had this to say about her support of National Public Radio and NPR's relevance to her as a Black American.

> "I support NPR with an annual gift of $360 a year. I love the stories and in-depth, behind-the-scenes reporting that you don't hear anywhere else, but on a personal note, I feel smarter and more knowledgeable. And as an African American this is important as well. I can plant seeds of information in my community, comfortably converse with different groups about current topics."

Anita supports two women every month through Women for Women

International an organization that gives aid and support to women who are survivors of war and personal atrocities. Anita's monthly support specifically goes to women in Congo and Rwanda where women learn new skills to support their families.

"I feel the need to support my Black community here in America through my church, the NAACP and Urban League, and in other countries as well," says Anita (who confessed that she, too, supports NPR).

There is a prevailing myth that African Americans don't give, only give to the church, or that we only give our time and not money," said Valaida Fullwood who spent over four years collecting stories, like those from Lauryn and Anita, from 200 Black Americans and authored *Giving Back: A Tribute to Generations of African-American Philanthropists* (John Blair, Publisher, 2011).

The coffee table–style book chronicles generations of the African-American philanthropy experience based on Fullwood's interviews with everyday people, with photos taken by photographer Charles Thomas.

Fullwood, a GenXer, explained that her Boomer parents grounded her in Black history. She listened to what they said, read what they shared, and saw how they lived, and realized that she needed to "counter those narratives" that society embraced about Black giving. *Giving Back* covers stories from a wide range of people—including many Black Boomers—from communities of people who have overcome hard times and still found ways to be charitable via myriad philanthropic practices grounded in faith, mutuality, and responsibility. One of the stories that stands out is Elizabeth Ross Dargan. She was a teacher retired from the Charlotte-Mecklenburg Schools who grew up in a rural North Carolina town and had a real commitment to giving. She gave to United Way campaigns and served on boards. When she passed, she bequeathed about a quarter of a million dollars to several nonprofits, including Charlotte's Urban League.[2]

Marketers are leaving dollars on the table by not talking directly to Black Boomers. In addition to Black Boomers' participation in philanthropic practices, here's some of what marketers are also missing.

African-American Boomers:

- Represent 23 percent of the African-American population, or 8.9 million people.

- Collectively, are the largest disposable-income group compared with any other African-American group, controlling over 30 percent of buying power ($298B).[3]

- Represent 40 percent of Black households having incomes between $50–$100K.

- Are 57 percent of Black homeowners, with 38 percent urban

- Very tech savvy—often first adapters. They are heavy purchasers of plasma TVs, PCs, high-speed internet with Wi-Fi and home theater systems.

- Heavy users of internet and mobile devices.

- As grandparents, provide shelter for grandchildren and their parents who often reside in the same household. In fact, the number of grandchildren being raised by grandparents or even great-grandparents is higher in this group than in any other major racial or ethnic group.

Marketers looking to take advantage of this often ignored and forgotten segment, should consider connecting with this segment in a relevant way. To grow their brand they should look at going "old school."

Notes

1. Empowerment Experiment: www.eefortomorrow.com
2. Annie Mojar, "Valaida Fullwood Gives Back," *Charlotte Magazine,* October, 2011.
3. Actwo Agency (projection based on estimates of Boomer data and 2009 African-American buying power).

Frustrated Black Boomer (and GenXer) Marketers Fill a Niche to Promote Black Consumer Power

In the Black ad community, there is a building movement among Boomer and some GenX executives to leverage information about the power and influence of Black consumers.

- Since the launch of *What's Black About It?* in 2005, there have been a number of books referencing Black consumer marketing and identity, such as *Brainwashed* by Tom Burrell, *Who's Afraid of Post-Blackness?* by Touré, *How to Be Black* by Baratunde Thurston, *Madison Avenue and the Color Line* by Dr. Jason Chambers, *Black is the New Green,* by Leonard E. Burnett and Andrea Hoffman; *Under the Influence: Tracing the Hip-Hop Generation's Impact on Brands, Sports, and Pop Culture,* by Erin O. Patton and *The 85% Niche,* by Miriam Muléy.

- In 2010 Jim Glover, Ted Pettus, and Paa Kwesi Adams launched the Actwo Agency that focuses on a forward thinking, highly evolved segment of Black Boomers.

- When *Ad Age* says no, KissMyBlackAds.com says yes. The KMBA BlogSpot was created by Craig Brimm, a GenXer who describes the platform as an "ultra-cultural" blog to "put a little paint where it ain't or to shine a favorable light on the more diverse dealings in the game."

- AABoomers.com is an online special-interest magazine targeted to the nearly 9 million African-American Baby Boomers.

- In 2011 the Cable Advertising Bureau (CAB) under the direction of Cynthia Perkins Roberts, VP of multicultural marketing, launched reachingBlackconsumers.com. It's been a long time coming for Perkins Roberts, the creative force behind the project. In addition to convincing the CAB that this was important, she enlisted 25 partnering companies—research companies, ad agencies and media companies, including yours truly—to contribute content for the site.

The efforts from these leaders speak to their tenacity to tell the Black consumer story despite years of being ignored, undervalued and misunderstood.

CHAPTER 10

Under the Radar:
Black Women

By Sarah Lattimer, CEO, Lattimer Communications

Here we are well into the new millennium, and yes, even with an African-American President and an intelligent and beautiful Black First Lady, change has been slow to come for Black women as it relates to marketing and advertising. Even though African-American women possess many of the traits that should make them attractive to most marketers, they are still underserved.

What's so special about Black women, you may ask? Easy. The numbers. There are over 22 million African-American women in the U.S.—approximately 55 percent of the Black population. They either influence or are responsible for over 85 percent of the purchasing decisions in their households. And, in 2009 Black women's spending power was estimated at over $565 billion and is predicted to double by 2014.

Many Black moms are different. Seventy-one percent of all Black births are to single moms[1] and these moms believe their life is different compared with single White moms. Black moms tend to be strict disciplinarians—not abusive, but many do spank. And many believe it is important to teach their children about the realities of life.

By the Numbers

Millions of Black Women Are on Their Own

42%	Black Women have never been married vs. 21% of White women
71%	Black births to single mothers vs. 53% of Latino, 29% of White and 17% of Asian moms

So why do some advertisers continuously overlook these women? One major *faux pas* is to mistakenly believe that Black women are the same as general-market women, so they approach both in the same way. Big mistake.

According to respondents to the 2010 *Essence* magazine survey of its readers, *The State of Black Women*:

- Black women continue to have a healthier view of themselves: 55% say they are sexy vs. 27% of White females.

- 85% date within their own race, and are two times more likely than White females to date someone of another race.

- Only 6% evaluate their success based on what others think vs. 11% of White females.

- Despite gender and racial barriers, Black women are better educated and earning more than ever.

- 567%: the increase in Black women completing college since 1960.

- $67,454 is the average household income for their readers, $16,867 less than that of White women.

- 58% of Black women work full-time outside the home.

- 49% of Black women report they are challenged by a lack of money; White women feel they don't have enough time.

- 16% of Black women are unemployed or stay-at-home moms.[2]

Many marketers also believe that showing a Black woman in an ad targeting the general market will suffice. Or they buy into the erroneous images of African-American women based upon the skewed, perverse, highly inaccurate, and often offensive depictions within visual media (news, TV, movies, music videos).

Lattimer Communications' study, *A Profile of Today's Black Woman* revealed that 86 percent of African-American women feel that advertisers do not know how to talk to them. Although most industries did not fare well, healthcare/pharmaceutical, automotive, financial services, travel, and fast food ranked the lowest. The study also identified six psychographic profiles of African-American women:

- Achievers
- Fledglings
- Tag-A-Longs
- Self-Sufficients
- Traditionals
- Cynics

The segments not only demonstrate how Black women are different from each other, but also reveal nuances and characteristics that serve as opportunities to connect with Black women. Here's a quick snapshot of two of the profiles.

The Achiever

Meet Valerie McMillon. She is an achiever. Her mantra is "The world is mine" and she represents approximately 23 percent of Black women. She is:

Confident: She's a risk taker, capable, and in some areas, an over-achiever. She is very proud and image and status conscious. Her physical appearance is extremely important to her.

Carefree Spender: She buys brands. She is not a bargain shopper.

Connected: She is heavily networked and involved in her community. She is always on the go.

A Caretaker: She is protective of her family, her community, and her culture. She believes it is important to set an example.

Here's an example of a day in the life of Valerie:

OK Diary. Today was pure fabulousness!!!

I went to that empowerment seminar and I tell you, it's just something about being in the company of so many intelligent Black women doing their thing, taking care of their families and looking fierce in the process. It took everything in me to stop checking out bags and shoes and actually focus on the speakers. They talked about health, spirituality, finances . . . you name it. There were a few audible groans when they mentioned cutting down on shopping, but I'm right where I need to be, on all fronts. Biodynamic was the new buzz word. I eat right but that's like next level organic. Might be too much work for me. I'll check out Wikipedia, do a couple of searches, see what I can find. Best believe I'll be on Bluefly in the morning, too. Ooh and I have to follow-up with all of my new contacts. I don't think I've ever seen so many Smartphones in one room in my life. When I finally take the entrepreneurial plunge, I'll have a great network on my already great network. Like that Verizon guy with all of the people behind him. A couple of the ladies were talking about going to some leadership summit in Palm Springs together. And you know me, I'm always down for a road trip. Stay tuned.

The Self-Sufficient

Now meet Jennifer Mathis, Self-Sufficient. Her mantra is: "I got this." She is:

Self-contained: And is most likely to be single.

Independent: Manages her own affairs.

Wired: Connected via online and social networking.

A Splurger: Buys what she wants, travels, and is brand conscious. But, she also saves and plans for retirement.

Read what Jennifer tells her Diary:

So I thought it was safe to leave my niece lying across my bed, engrossed in watching, for the 20th time, *The Princess and the Frog*. I am so happy that little Summer finally has a princess that she can identify with. Me too.

Imagine my surprise when I came back less than five minutes later and found her in my closet, playing dress-up in Auntie's Louboutins. Are you kidding me? I told her that SHE was going to have a red bottom if she didn't take them off pronto. Of course I was joking. Well, sort of. LOL! As much as I enjoy spending time with her, and her insatiable curiosity, that was one more reminder as to why I won't be ready for kids any time soon.

And If I had to hear "Why?" one more time . . .

I don't know how moms do it. I think I just enjoy my independence more than the average person. I go where I want, do what I like, spend as much as I please and most importantly don't have to answer to anyone, little, or big for that matter.

Don't get me wrong I look forward to finding "the one" someday. That's why I joined match.com. I practically live online anyway. Who knows all of the business I do on LinkedIn, might even lead to some pleasure.

But in the meantime, I'm quite content and can do for myself. I like that I know how to change my own oil, fix a flat and build a deck if I want to. THANK YOU DIY (Do-It-Yourself) network!!!!! And that's a side I'm proud to share with my niece. See, my sister and I are two very different people. As much as she loves her "traditional" mom, I think it's healthy for her to experience a variety of women in different roles. So at the end of the day, I guess I should be flattered that she wanted to walk in my shoes, literally or figuratively."

As you can see, although these two women are similar in some respects, they approach life quite differently. It is essential for marketers to understand not only these two types of Black women but also to get to know the other four as well. Advertisers will find that by identifying the target profile, they will better understand the intricacies and nuances of their desired customer and thus reap better results. Connecting with Black women can create a highly profitable and long-term relationship. And that's the point, isn't it?

Pine-Sol Powerful Difference
Celebrating the Strength of Black Women

The Powerful Difference™ program, started by Pine-Sol in 2007, believes in the strength of the everyday woman in the Black community. When women unite there is strength to make a powerful force for transformation in their societies.

Powerful Difference supports and develops positive change where it exists. It helps create those forces of change where needed. Powerful Difference gives women tools—scholarships, cash grants, workshops, and websites—and inspiration to go into their neighborhoods and be that difference.

Sisterspeak® luncheons, presented in partnership with *Ebony* magazine, have been hosted in cities across the country with major Black populations. The luncheons join several hundred women with motivational keynote speakers to animate their visions. Sisterspeak luncheons also honor those African-American women who have already become catalysts for change in their environments. Make a Powerful Difference Action Kits assist in project maintenance and development using a five-pronged attack plan featuring guidelines to help women, groups, and communities in organizing, fundraising, educating, volunteering and mentoring. This translates to hundreds and hundreds of women supporting women, and women and communities supporting the brand.

There's a Facebook page with thousands of "likes" and The Powerful Difference website links to others that offer locations where groups can help within their cities and neighborhoods. Inspirational videos of Sisterspeak luncheons and stimulating women of action are featured here, too.

Within each woman is the power to make a positive difference; Pine-Sol knows it and shows it.

Source: Powerfuldifference.com

Accomplished Young Black Women
The New "She-ros" and Influencers

- Today's young accomplished Black women (aged 23 to 37) are indepen-dent, place a higher value on education than ever before, and under-stand the connection between higher education and the potential for success that it provides.

- They are ambitious and restless, and tend to change jobs more frequent-ly than previous generations.

- Young Black women are considering self-employment and business ownership at a higher rate than ever, and have driven much of the growth in Black entrepreneurship, up nearly 75% in recent years.[3]

- At the same time, these women are, or will likely become, the primary decision makers or heads of households in their daily lives. They are future purchasers of their own homes and cars, and will be, at the very least, co-decision makers for all medical, educational, and financial op-tions for themselves and their families, and possibly their aging parents.

- Additionally, many are delaying, or foregoing, childbearing at a higher rate. In 2008, 1.7 million Black women aged 20 to 34 (39%) had no chil-dren vs. 1.46 million, or 34%, childless Black women in 2003.

- Young women have a preference for Black advertising and insist on authenticity and respond more favorably to products that are used by Hip-Hop artists or celebrities prior to their becoming a brand spokesper-son.[4] In other words, they want to discover "cool" for themselves, rather than be told what is cool.

- This group ranks high on the scale of "consumerism" and spends money on electronics, cars, and fashion. They are also more likely to buy treats or gifts for themselves such as manicures and spa visits, or to go out with friends for cocktails or dinner.[5]

Researched and prepared by Jacklynn J. Topping

Notes

1. Lyndra Vassar, "BHM: The State of African-American Women," www.essence. com, September 2010.

2. J. Hopkins, "Black Women Step Up in the Business World," *Miami Times,* April, 2008.

3. "The Young Urban Consumer Market in the U.S.," *Packaged Facts,* 2008.

4. Karlene Lukovitz, "Trend-setting Hip-Hoppers Are Aging, but Are Brand-Loyal as Ever," *www.Mediapost.com,* May 9, 2008.

5. Sam Roberts, "Birthrate Falls for Whites to About Half," *New York Times,* May 6, 2010.

CHAPTER 11

Under the Radar:
Blacks and the Green Movement

Speaking of carbon footprints, non-renewable energy, sustainability and compost piles might bring shrugs or looks of puzzlement to many. Attempting to understand the complexities associated with the Green Movement can be overwhelming and off-putting. To understand that the same government that positioned garbage dumps next to public housing and drove small, rural farmers out of business, is now the government that will restore the country's infrastructure and create jobs in the Black communities, is one of the challenges and opportunities grass roots activists face while encouraging Blacks to get involved in the Green Movement.

Thus, for many African Americans, "green" engagement must have a personal connection to them and be relevant to their community.

Using (and reusing) what you have to extend your own resources is not a message that African Americans own, but mention hand-me-downs, and getting greens and tomatoes from your back yard vegetable garden to eliminate food deserts—another reality in the inner city—and the Green Movement takes on new meaning. For many years the African-American community has passed down and made do with whatever they had. In a culture where the décor of an entire home might consist of the table from Aunt May and the sofa from Sandy because she just got a new one, Black people know well about reusing products that still have value.

Addressing issues at the neighborhood level is Majora Carter, a MacArthur Foundation "genius" grant winner, who explains to folks in locations like the South Bronx how the green economy and jobs such as installing solar panels, building the national grid or restoring wetlands can save the planet and significantly reduce Black unemployment levels; global warming is not only something one may see on the evening news. More than $400 million in Sustainable Communities grants were handed out in 2010, much of which goes directly toward addressing environmental issues in low-income communities.[1]

Jamal Ali, author of *Black and Green: Black Insights for the Green Movement,* connects the Black experience with green initiatives in a very serious, yet sometimes lighthearted, way and presents strategies and rationales for African Americans to participate in the green movement. An example of how this connection is made is with vacant lots, which are plentiful in most Black neighborhoods. He says these lots can be converted to community gardens where the entire neighborhood can help plant and maintain the garden and suggests that if more Black people got involved in rediscovering their neighborhoods—invoking green initiatives in the process—crime would actually decrease.

Ali is encouraged by some initiatives and changes that both directly and indirectly affect the Black community:

> "I am finding more and more Black people that have been involved in the green movement for quite some time. . . . Schools are educating [Black] students on climate change and words like 'food deserts' are being tossed around more."

While the connection between market gardens vs. food deserts clicks, it's difficult for most to see how being market gardeners again and shopping at Goodwill instead of Lord & Taylor's make for good, green citizens. The easiest way to connect African Americans to the Green Movement is to demonstrate how these policies and practices can be of practical and fiscal benefit to the Black community. Grassroots advocates like Naomi Davis, president of Chicago-based, BIG (Blacks in Green) educates Black communities about environmental consequences, business opportunities, civic activism, and healthier lifestyles.

As African-American environmental justice proponents Van Jones and Phaedra Ellis-Lamkins will tell you, though clean energy is a less obvious racial issue than, say, education or criminal justice, it's becoming increasingly evident that what goes into our water and air, and how we build our energy infrastructure, are, or should be, topics of grave importance to African Americans.[2]

Notes

1. Cord Jefferson, "How Obama's Green Policies Benefit Blacks," *The Root*, October 29, 2010.
2. Ibid.

CHAPTER 12

Making a Connection

1. Black America Wants You *to Want* to Get Black Culture

If you really want to change, announce to the world that you want to change . . . We have to look at how the world has changed and match up to it.

—Larry Woodard, CEO, Graham Stanley Advertising

There is a scene in the 2006 movie *The Break Up* starring Vince Vaughn as Gary and Jennifer Aniston as Brooke, where we see the couple arguing. Gary won't help Brooke with the dishes following a dinner party in which Brooke did all of the work. After several selfish reasons and snarky comments as to why he shouldn't do the dishes, Gary reluctantly gives in. But Brooke backs up and declines his help and tells him, "I want you to *want* to do the dishes."

I love that line and totally get it! It's the same with connecting with Black America.

No group wants to force another group to appreciate their culture and who they are—they simply want that group to want to appreciate it. Just like Brooke in the movie, it is a matter of respect more than the actually doing.

In order for a Black consumer marketing effort to be successful, it is essential to come to the table with the right attitude. Marketers first must *want to* want to get Black culture. When marketers have little or no interest, no curiosity, no passion, and no commitment to Black culture, it will show; both short term and long term efforts are bound to fail.

Consumers of all races take pleasure in inviting you into their personal culture. It is who they are and what they believe.

You would not go to a person's house and insult and degrade the items in the home that represent their family and culture. Marketers must understand that not accepting the invitation to better understand and appreciate someone else's culture is the same form of disrespect.

Showing an appreciation for another group's culture can not only increase sales. In addition, it can create a customer base that is more likely to remain loyal through both good and bad times.

Marketers must want to want to get Black culture. And when they do, the marketing and advertising will develop a voice that resonates.

2. Understand the Value of Respect

Despite all the progress that's been made, there's still a nagging sense of being looked down upon, of being judged, of being disrespected. What keeps this difference alive is that these suspicions aren't always paranoia.

> —Eugene Robinson, Pulitzer Prize–winning columnist, *Washington Post*, and author, *Disintegration: The Splintering of Black America*

Respect (really) matters.

During the summer of 2007 while on one of my business trips, I made an impromptu stop in Nashville to visit a good friend. While heading to the gym one morning, my friend and I stopped at a national department store to pick up a houseware item. The store had just opened. There were only a few shoppers milling around.

I had not planned to shop, but on the way to housewares, I was delighted to see select men's designer suits marked down to a very attractive price. The bargain hunter in me couldn't resist. As my interest in the suits peaked, a sales associate approached me. He was not rude, but in a nearly empty store he was indifferent toward my friend and me and was unavailable for the majority of my shopping time.

For over 30 minutes, with the help of my friend and her daughter,

I fumbled through the process of selecting three suits for my husband and one for my dad. I made it to the counter, not feeling great about the sales associate getting credit for the sale, but I was so happy with "my find" that I didn't want to make his indifference a big deal. Because I had been traveling on business and had not anticipated coming to Nashville, let alone doing some shopping, I had limited luggage space. I asked the sales associate to waive the $14-per-item shipping fee (given my status as a VIP customer, this fee has been waived at other stores in other cities under the same store brand).

Before I could blink, he flatly said "No."

I mentioned that I was an Elite customer, and explained that the fee at other stores has been waived before.

Still, "No."

I then asked if he would get permission from the manager on duty who was in view with a clipboard, checking stock. The associate walked over to the sales manager who looked past the associate to me. I saw the manager mouth the words to the sales associate, "Tell her no."

Not only was I was surprised with his answer, but also that he didn't come over to personally speak with me. My girlfriend's Millennial-aged daughter quickly rationalized the incident by saying, "Aunt Pepper, this is the South."

My friend clarified her daughter's comment by attributing our poor service to being African American and wearing gym attire.

"C'mon," I responded, "it's 2007!! If White females who are dressed for the gym, and shop at this store expect good service, do African Americans have to dress a particular way for the same service?"

Puzzled and not feeling like a valued customer, I immediately left the suits on the counter and the store wondering to myself, is this happening because I'm Black or are these guys jerks? Do they treat everyone like this? To be honest, I wouldn't have minded paying the shipping if I absolutely had to, but neither the sales associate nor the manager seemed to care whether the store got my business.

I sent a letter to the regional vice president and store manager. They responded via phone and a letter to let me know both employees had been fired. I don't believe the employee firing was from my incident alone, but rather from that inevitable "straw." Nonetheless, that experience stayed with me for a long, long time. As a child, I lived with my family for a few years in the pre–Civil Rights south. That behavior wasn't new. I know that experience. I know the feeling. And it *still* hurt.

In 1995, Yankelovich conducted a survey among Black and White shoppers to determine their primary reasons for department store selection. Twelve years later, in 2007, a major national department store conducted a customer satisfaction survey, and asked the same questions. Two separate surveys, with two different audiences and within two different timelines, revealed "price" was the number one answer for both Black and White shoppers. However, "the availability of merchandise" was the number two response from White shoppers, but for Black shoppers the number two answer was "Respect."

Peering through the lens of the pre– and post–Civil Rights Eras has caused many African Americans to place a value on being respected. This value is the most important, most enlightening, and most overarching cultural marketing insight for understanding Black America.

Here's another example from a different angle. Consider the marketer who uses a traditional one-size-fits-all approach for reaching all moms. He or she will surely miss the opportunity to tap into "respect" as an integral value for rearing Black children. For example, Black moms are more likely than White moms to use corporal punishment to discipline their children. This practice was particularly obvious when observing separate focus groups of Black and White parents during a 2007 qualitative study for a government agency.

In addition to the separate parent groups, we conducted separate focus groups of the parents' teen-age children. Black teens and their parents openly discussed the use of corporal punishment in their households (with these parents often associating this punishment with the slang reference "the beat down") as well as restricting a variety of privileges.

Few White parents indicated that they used corporal punishment as a disciplinary tactic. Instead, they indicated that they are more likely to talk through issues with their children and restrict privileges.

Additionally, after exposing a TV ad to these parents, which features a loving Black father reprimanding his daughter in front of her friends when she disobeyed him, most White parents were completely turned off ("I'd never embarrass my child in front of his/her friends!") whereas Black parents cheered the father character on.

Black parents are also more likely to teach their children to respect their elders and not question authority (50 percent vs. 33 percent for White parents). Finally, Black parents are more likely to make sure that children address non-relative adults as "Mr. Miller" or "Miss Jackie" or "Aunt Pepper" and "Uncle Ron," rather than by their first names, particularly if the adults are close to the family. It's simply a matter of respect.

Although this custom has some socio-economic and generational implications, overall it is more a more widespread practice among Blacks than Whites.

It doesn't cost much to give respect but in the Black community it can pay high dividends for a marketer who recognizes its power and influence.

Respecting Black Consumers through Recognition

365 Black: McDonald's Program
Recognizes Black History Everyday

In the Black community it's heard all the time—"Black History Month is February and it's the shortest month in the year!" and "How come we only get one month?"

McDonald's Corporation paid attention and responded to the voices in "the hood."

365Black.com is McDonald's internet celebration of African Americans each and every day of the year. This is the place where information and accolades appear. All things African American connected to the McDonald's operation and under its umbrella are noted here.

The website is a place of user-friendly pages of encouraging words, events, and opportunities for business, employment and education. McDonald's has supported events including the Essence Music Festival, the Inspiration Celebration Gospel Tour and the HBCU Football Classic, in several cities annually. The 365Black Awards ceremony continues to honor outstanding community service given by talented and dedicated women and men of color.

The focus of the website is what McDonald's does for the community and how African Americans may continue to benefit from this long-term, ongoing relationship with the golden arches. 365Black.com is a demonstration and an example of the commitment one corporate entity displays to its consumers.[1]

———

General Mills' Feeding Dreams

"There are thousands of Black people doing great things for their communities and for too long these stories have gone unnoticed until Feeding Dreams."

—Sandra Jones, CEO, SMSi

A champion is a winner and a defender. Since 2008 several General Mills brands have honored Community Champions with their Feeding Dreams campaign. In each of ten southern cities community "she-ros" and heroes are nominated by friends and family. Contestants are selected for their active roles in improving conditions at the grassroots level in ten urban African-American communities. Feeding Dreams selects one champion from the nominees for each city. One of these ten is chosen by votes received from the community at large to be Grand Champion. The Champions' caring spirits and hard work are rewarded with prizes to their charity plus a small personal monetary award for each entrant.

GM believes in acknowledging the hard work and dedication of the women and men who believe in themselves and their neighbors. Programs developed by champions include youth mentoring, volunteer training, creating support networks for troubled individuals and much more. Feeding Dreams outreach continues to grow. Originally in four cities the contest has expanded to include Birmingham, Columbia, Jackson, Jacksonville, New Orleans, Norfolk, Memphis, Miami and Charlotte. Awards to charities and Champions have also increased since the program began.

The Feeding Dreams website assists in helping to feed a community larger than the 10 Champion cities. In addition to articles on past Champions, the site gives tips and guidelines on education, lifestyle and well being. This even includes product coupons and recipes.

General Mills encourages its employees to give their time and talent to their local communities. GM demonstrates the same commitment by creating programs like Feeding Dreams. In recognizing and assisting the dreams, General Mills does feed dreams.

3. Know Who You Are Really Talking To

Today there are many ways to be Black in America.

Although still a bit slow out of the gate, society is finally coming around to recognize that all Blacks are not the same. There's no one monolithic way to speak to, interact with, and hold a conversation with Black America.

The fact is that compared to any other time in history, Blacks today are more different from each other in very meaningful ways.

An insightful example of how Blackness is different for many Black Americans, is Professor Michael Eric Dyson and Touré's discussion and outline of three dimensions of Blackness in Touré's newest book, *Who's Afraid of Post-Blackness? What it Means to Be Black Now,* in which Touré, a journalist, writer, and MSNBC contributor—examines modern Black identity. Dyson and Touré agree on the definitions of these dimensions, but have different names for each.

Michael Eric Dyson and Touré: Three Primary Dimensions of Blackness[1]

Dyson	Touré	Explanation
Accidental	Introverted	Private relationship with Blackness. "I am American. I am human."
Incidental	Ambiverted	Completely embrace Blackness but it does not dominate their persona
Intentional	Extroverted	Strong Black association

Dyson, professor at Georgetown University, author of several books, radio host and commentator on National Public Radio, CNN, and MSNBC, reminds us that most Blacks do not necessarily remain in these dimensions all the time. Depending on the situation, many weave in and out of these dimensions as needed. Dyson explains:

"... confining most people within one of these modes isn't easy. Different moments present different situations that demand that we modulate. . . . Black people have different modes of Blackness and when we need to be each of those varieties of Blackness we exercise them. . . . When you (Blacks) deal with multiple audiences, you (Blacks) have to pivot around different presentations of Blackness."[2]

Thus, understanding how, where, and why Blacks fall into particular segments is essential for improving one's African-American cultural IQ. For marketers, it's critical toward the development of effective market plans, strategies and communications.

Pulitzer Prize–winning columnist for the *Washington Post*, Eugene Robinson, brings the attention of Black segmentation to the mainstream with his book, *Dis-Integration: The Splintering of Black America*. Robinson's tome is a nice complement to the segmentation studies conducted by respected media and communications companies because it illuminates the historical back story behind his four well-defined segments: Mainstream Middle Class, the large Abandoned Minority, the Transcendent Elite, and two Emergent groups: individuals of mixed-race heritage and recent Black immigrants (African and Caribbean).

To illustrate how Black America has divided, let's examine the real lifestyles of four Millennial Black men—Christopher, Michael, Randall, and Dante.

Marketers are in love with Millennials. They are the go-to segment for many marketers. When you consider the group's age range, size, trending characteristics both as influencers and as followers, and most importantly, buying power, it is easy to see why. Millennials represent a powerful segment of the population, and yet young Black men, despite their influence in the Black community and pop culture, are virtually ignored by marketers.

Christopher and Michael are each age 27. Although their mothers are best friends and have known each other since grade school, Christopher and Michael are cordial, but not close. They do share some things in common: both enjoy connecting with friends on Facebook, traveling within the U.S. to visit friends, party, ski, and hike. They also enjoy visiting various locations in Mexico and the Caribbean.

Despite everything they have in common, Christopher and Michael live parallel lifestyles but in vastly different worlds.

Christopher grew up in a White, middle class, suburban community. He attended predominately White schools through college, and has very few (if any) Black friends. When he and his close friends get together, they resemble a delegation from the United Nations. Christopher has comfortably adapted to the culture of his environment. Those in Christopher's circle genuinely like and respect him, and are happy to share friendships with him. At the same time, Christopher is often the poster boy for post-racial rhetoric. He's society's example of "the end of racism" and, at the firm where he works, Christopher is the go-to Black person for internal and external communication checks to ensure that messages resonate with the Black community at large. While Christopher acknowledges his race, he feels it plays less of a role in his world. He believes those around him see him as Christopher first and not "Christopher the Black guy."

Michael grew up Black middle class. He attended Black grade schools and high school and graduated from an HBCU (Historically Black College and University). Michael's parents constantly exposed him to diverse groups and made sure he had balanced experiences outside the Black community, yet Michael has very few (if any) White friends. His "boys" are college graduates and are also Black. Michael has collaborated with a few like-minded friends to create an events company that hosts parties and social events all over the country and the Caribbean. Be it a beach party and concert in Aruba, a ski trip to Vail, or a series of high-end events on yachts and other exclusive venues, you will find Michael and his partners mingling and networking with hundreds of young Black professionals. They gather these groups primarily from Twitter, Facebook, e-blasts and word-of-mouth. Michael doesn't see a separation between his race and who he is. He seeks out ways to incorporate his culture and heritage into all aspects of his life. He consciously chooses to maintain a strong connection to the Black community. He is proud of his race, and feels it is a part of what makes him Michael.

Randall has a foot in both worlds. Raised in a close-knit family, his main focus is on family and friends. His Facebook friends are about 50 percent Black and 50 percent White. He grew up in a Black community and attended an Ivy League university. He pledged a Black fraternity, and was an officer in the student government association. He describes himself as diverse, with a Black consciousness. Randall and his wife, Anna, are successful entrepreneurs, who live in a diverse community with their young daughter. They want their daughter to be exposed to different cultures, but also are also teaching her about Black culture. They spend lots of time with family, especially during birthdays and holidays. They also love to entertain and enjoy traveling with their close friends who are a diverse group. Randall doesn't see a need to live in one world or the other; he is perfectly comfortable moving between the two. He believes that the two worlds can mix, and doesn't see a reason why they shouldn't.

Dante, 21, grew up in a single parent household. His mother raised him and his younger brother on a clerical worker's salary in a stable lower-middle class neighborhood. Dante wasn't a bad kid but has experienced the consequences of making wrong choices. In spite of his troubles, Dante rebounded and graduated from high school. Dante is also a father. He has one young child and is not in a relationship with his child's mother, but is trying to do the right thing by them both. He works full-time and lives with his mom. Dante's world is insular and familiar, yet he feels good about his life. He works, shares custody of his son, hangs out with his friends and has a new girlfriend. He has dreams of owning his own business, but is not quite sure what that business would be. Dante is comfortable in his world, seeing no reason to live outside of it. He doesn't view it as a choice based on race as much as one of familiarity. He is comfortable and happy in the world he has grown up in. He doesn't embrace his race as much as he lives it.

In spite of their differences, all four are digitally savvy. They enjoy being first among their friends to own the latest technology, and own one or more of the following: smartphones, MP3s, iPods, tablets, laptop and desk top computers, video games, etc. They have tons of friends on Facebook, but in general, use different media. They all have active Twitter accounts although the subjects of their Tweets vary.

Christopher and Michael are online 24/7. They keep abreast of current issues via local TV news, mainstream magazines—both from subscriptions and online—and popular online news resources like CNN.

Michael is also more likely than Christopher to devote time connecting with Black culture via urban news and entertainment websites and music and lifestyle blogs such as: rapradar, nahright, singleBlackmale, verysmartbrothas, nowness, theurbandaily, and theroot.

Christopher reads lots of mainstream blogs, likes Anime (Japanese animation) and watches Comedy Central, the Syfy Channel, and *American Idol.*

Randall consumes a variety of media that is equally split between mainstream and Black content. He feels both are equally important for staying informed.

Dante watches a lot of television and gets his news from late night local news. He also listens to the radio in the car, and at home—in his room and throughout the house via his mother's select radio stations.

Michael and Dante are also frequent viewers of TV One and BET. *Martin* reruns is a favorite on TV One, and both are fans of BET's comedy/drama *The Game.* They are fans of anything that has a connection to the Hip-Hop community but do not limit their viewing to that.

Four Black men. Four different lifestyles. Four different media habits. Yes, they speak English, but are you sure you're talking to them?

For younger generations, when it comes to mass advertising, tapping into cultural cues now means: "Is the commercial funny, entertaining, or creative?" "Does it make me like the brand or product even more?" Many young African Americans also express a disdain for advertising that overtly emphasizes African-American cultural cues as these cues begin to feel like stereotypes versus connectors, and will kill your message very quickly. So the question becomes, do I lump the young African-American consumer into all of my general market outreach? The answer is yes and no. When it comes to placement and online engagement you must have a targeted approach and show a deeper understanding of a particular segment's culture. The end game for all marketers in this social media age should be a strong relationship between brands and their consumers—it's all about **connection**. It is also about inspiring people to **share** through social media. For African-American youth (and all African Americans) it means so much more for marketers to show love in a way that is appealing to their mindset, class, social media networks and chosen mediums.

Who Are You Really Talking To?

	Christopher Accidental/ Introverted	Michael Intentional/ Extroverted	Randall Incidental/ Ambiverted	Dante Incidental/ Ambirverted
Community raised in/resides in	Predominately White	Black/Urban	Black/Urban	Black/Urban
Closest friends	Diverse; mostly White	Mostly Black	Diverse; split equally between Black and White	Mostly Black
Digitally Savvy: Frequent use of the latest computers, smartphones, iPods, MP3s, video games	Among first to own the latest technology	Among first to own the latest technology	Among first to own the latest technology	Among first to own the latest technology
Visits Black news and entertainment sites	Rarely to not at all	Frequently	Sometimes	Rarely
Importance of Black advertising	Less important	Very important	Very important	Somewhat important

4. Leverage Opportunities Under the Radar

The value of a group isn't related to its size, a group's value is related to its influence.
                                   —Seth Godin, author, *Purple Cow*

For most marketers, better success has been hiding in plain sight. Recognizing the segments inside the African-American community that traditionally have been ignored or taken for granted can be an important coup for marketers and incremental earnings to their bottom line. As discussed eariler, these segments include Black men, Black immigrants, Black biracials, Black LGBTs, Black Boomers, Black women, and Blacks and the Green Movement.

Notes

1. Touré, *Who's Afraid of Post-Blackness? What It Means to Be Black Now* (New York: Free Press, 2011).
2. Ibid.

Engaging Black Youth:
It's All About Connection

By Kevin Walker, CEO, CultureLab

Three years ago I wrote and posted an article, "Rise of The Black Hipsters," that documented what was then an emerging trend of young Black kids dressing like and mimicking the lifestyle of White urban hipsters from the Williamsburg section of Brooklyn, New York. My company, CultureLab, has also documented the adaptation of White west coast skater culture on urban youth. This is what we call "reverse appropriation." Identity in some instances has morphed from purely racial to race and an individual's lifestyle, i.e., skaters, crunkfeminists, hipsters, bohos, and so on. There is a proliferation of these tribes that has occurred and the question becomes "how do I reach them?"

Often, companies default to Hip-Hop cues in an attempt to market to African-American youth but times have changed. Hip-Hop is still a viable cornerstone of urban/African-American culture, especially among the underclass, but it is not the focal point it once was. It could be argued that technology culture has supplanted Hip-Hop as the key movement of this time. This is the age of mobile tech, video games, Twitter, YouTube, crossover music, and the creation of online content: videos, tweets, and blog postings. Technology defines African-American Millennial culture just as it does for their counterparts of other ethnicities.

The online world facilitates connection to other like-minded individuals and groups thus deepening the connection around these interests. There is irony, however, in that for younger African Americans, race is less at the forefront in their online life; yet offline, the majority live in segregated all-Black worlds.

Here are a set of questions marketers should answer before they develop strategic plans for targeting next-generation African Americans:

- Where does the target dwell: what region, urban and suburban?

- What tribe are they a part of: gamers, skaters, ballers, tuners, DUB gurus, thugsters, and hipsters?

- What is their social class? What mobile devices do they prefer?

- How do they consume media?

- Why do they share certain content on social networks? What social networks do they prefer?

- Who is the influencer of the tribe? What is their digital behavior? What is their offline behavior?

––––––

Major Studies Validate the Diversity of Black America

Four major segmentation studies launched between 2008 and 2010 confirm how Black America is changing:

- **The Black America Study,** the largest segmentation study to date, included 3,400 African Americans aged 13 to 74. Commissioned by Radio One and conducted by Yankelovich Partners, the 2008 study revealed 11 distinct segments of Black America.

- **African Americans Revealed** (2009 and 2011) was conducted among African Americans aged 14 to 55. The beauty of these two studies is that BET Networks analyzed the segmentation data with more than 80,000 consumers in their research panel to understand the values, interests and lifestyles of African Americans and the relationship to their personal aspirations, family structures, media preferences and product consumption.

- Starcom Media Vest Group's **Beyond Demographics** gathered information from more than 1,000 African Americans across the U.S., and from this data, pinpointed 12 profiles ranging from Trustees and Gazelles to Devouts and Thrivals, which the firm believes illustrates the rich diversity that exists within the Black community.

- Lattimer Communications created six psychographic profiles of African-American women via its study **A Profile of Today's Black Woman**. "These six profiles—Achievers, Fledglings, Tag-A-Longs, Self-Sufficients, Traditionals, and Cynics—are proof that Black women are, in fact, multi-dimensional," says Sarah Lattimer, CEO of Lattimer Communications.

––––––

CHAPTER 13

Black Media Matter:
Old Rules Don't Apply

By Pepper Miller with Kevin Walker, CEO, CultureLab

In the post–Civil Rights Era, from the late 1960s to the 1970s, there was a sprouting Black consciousness that drove many developments in politics, culture, advertising, and media. There was the rise of Black-owned Black hair care companies, increasing Black political gains, the prominence of *Soul Train*, the explosion of Blaxploitation films, and Black publications like *Ebony, Essence, Jet,* and *Black Enterprise.*

Compared with today, targeting Black consumers was a less compli-cated exercise: create soulful ads or content that tapped into the Black-pride mindset, run them on *Soul Train*, place print ads in the popular Black magazines and newspapers, buy spot radio, schedule and post billboards in Black neighborhoods, and you were pretty much covered.

Fast-forward to today, there's a sense of overwhelming complexity given that media dynamics now include online and offline attitudes, behavior, and experiences.

The misstep by many marketers is to fail to understand that African Americans, both young and old are also seeking and developing deeper connections with people like them in both online and offline media environments. Black Americans use general market media, but embrace Black media. Being comfortable with diverse media does not mean the abandonment of Black media. It's not one or the other, but both. Tar-geted media engagement means showing overtly that you are seeking a connection to particular consumer groups in their native settings, social media networks, and through their preferred entertainment. Thus, the key ingredients for a potent African-American marketing brew are relevant narratives across multiple media platforms including social media, traditional media (radio, TV, and print), online video, mobile applications, and experiential.

Black Media Today

In 2010, the African-American media experienced the same kinds of challenges and changes that mainstream news organizations also faced:[1]

- African-American newspapers, now mostly weeklies, moved in different directions, but those innovating with new sections and coverage did increase their circulation.

- Most of the major magazines had flat or reduced circulations, but the advertising picture was more promising. Some major publications had double-digit gains in ad pages after a difficult 2009.

- Online, the digital gap separating African Americans from other ethnic groups is closing and various publishers are looking to electronic tablets as the next frontier.

- In television, two of the largest cable channels geared to Black audiences now air weekly news talk shows, a shift in the last year.

- In radio, the biggest African American–focused broadcaster saw its stock delisted on the Nasdaq exchange but managed to restructure and restore its stock price to a level that met the exchange's standards.

Nonetheless, these changes and challenges have not caused Black audiences to abandon Black media. The opportunity for marketers is to understand how, why, and where these media fit into the lives and lifestyles of Black America today.

Black Newspapers: "Making Sure We're Not Silent"[2]

"There will always be an appetite and a market for [the Black press]," said media columnist Richard Prince. "People tend to see things that they don't see anywhere else. And just as important, they're written with the point of view that people can relate to."

The point that Prince makes above—"people . . . see things that they don't see anywhere else"—continues to be an important one for Black print media, and it continues to be taken lightly or is dismissed by advertisers. From early 2009 to early 2010, Pew Research's Project for Excellence in Journalism conducted a study on the coverage of Black Americans in the mainstream press and learned that as a group, African Americans attracted relatively little attention in the U.S. mainstream news cycle that year.

Like most newspapers that face declines in readership, Black newspapers particularly struggle with their reason for being. But many are determined to hold on and have experienced success with new strategies that include partnerships, having a strong online presence, creative events, and turning to experts that can provide relevant content. Examples of publications that used and benefited from these ideas follow.

- The LA newspaper, *Our Weekly,* was formed in 2004 as a means to reach the affluent African-American communities of Los Angeles, and recently expanded to Antelope Valley. It has a strong online as well as print presence, and reports local, statewide and national news stories. Its modern, news-oriented website helps attract a younger target, aged 25–54 years (vs. 35+ for other local newspapers), according to Alex Schildkret, director of advertising. It boasts readership of about 200,000.

- *South Florida Times,* a weekly with a circulation of 20,000, partnered with the Census Bureau and the University of Miami. The partnerships between ethnic media outlets and the Census Bureau vary from buying ad space in a newspaper to providing journalists with information for stories on the communities they cover. The Census

Bureau's effort to work with ethnic media comes out of fears that ethnic communities were undercounted in the 2000 Census. In Florida, for example, an estimated 200,000 people reportedly were not counted. "This relationship is such a success because it really connects the U.S. Census with key players of the minority media," said Helda M. Silva, a representative from the bureau who also worked as vice president of news for Univision and Telefutura in Miami and New York.[3]

- *The Chicago Defender* did not use the words "Negro" or "Black" in its pages when Robert Sengstacke Abbott founded the publication in 1905. Instead, African Americans were referred to as "the Race" and Black men and women as Race men and Race women. Today, the publication is owned by Real Times Media, a multimedia company with enterprises and interests including the most extensive African-American newspaper collective in the nation. Its papers include *The Michigan Chronicle; The Michigan Front Page; The New Pittsburgh Courier,* and the *Tri-State Defender* (Memphis), and it continues with that high level of integrity through its Men of Excellence and Women of Excellence events. These events honor local African-American men and women in business who have made significant contributions to the Black community. *The Defender* builds relationships with the people it honors and sells a boatload of ads to corporate sponsors, and awardees and event guests who support the publication with advertising purchases or subscriptions.

- "Providing provocative news, empowering information, that's unapologetically Black," is the slogan of the Trice-Edney News Wire Service, founded by Hazel Trice-Edney in 2010. Out of concern for struggling Black papers, Trice-Edney used her 25-years experience in the Black Press, her time as the Washington correspondent for the news service of the National Newspaper Publishers Association, and her former service as NNPA's editor-in-chief to develop a business that provides nationally focused and Black-oriented news stories, investigative reports, and opinion columns to more than 1,000 newspapers, radio stations and websites around the nation, all of which are either Black-owned, serve vast Black audiences, or are specifically interested in Black-oriented content.[4]

- Just twelve years ago, *Rolling Out* launched with one paper in one market. Today, it circulates 1.2 million copies of the weekly publication that features profiles of local urban executives, thought leaders, and entertainers. The newspaper is distributed in 19 of the top 25 African-American markets and is but one of the many media products under the Steed Media Group, headed by its founder and CEO, Munson Steed. Steed was way ahead of the curve and was poised to meet the changing needs of the consumer by building a conglomerate of media vehicles that he describes as a" 360-degree integrated engagement of the urban consumer." These vehicles include newspapers, event promotions, video branded content, and special events such as Seeding Minds, a youth literacy initiative that drives more than 60 percent of its traffic to rollingout.com.

  "African Americans on the whole are invisible. There's a clear cut meaning and responsibility for me as a publisher to service the community—to deliver a level of competency, give them access to talent, and to love them in a meaningful way," says Steed.

- Danny Bakewell, Sr., as publisher of both the *Los Angeles Sentinel* and the *LA Watts Times*, has implemented blogging, more opinion writing, and, at this writing, is planning on reorganizing its leadership. People turn to his papers, said Bakewell, "because they give those readers perspectives on the news that no one else will give." Bakewell adds, "People buy Black newspapers for a very simple reason: We want to see ourselves, in terms of getting a perspective of what's happening in the world and how we're playing into that. That becomes the epic value of the Black press. We're making sure we're not silent."[5]

Black Magazines

In spite of the challenges surrounding Black magazines, new magazine launches continue to happen locally and regionally. From 2002 to 2006 alone, 85 magazines that targeted African Americans were launched. These new magazines represent a mix of categories and interest, from fashion, beauty, and grooming to music, business, finance, and pop culture. In fact, the total number of magazine titles specifically targeting Black readers has consistently remained above 100 since 1996.[6]

Two of the newest publications, *Jones* and *Uptown*, have become major players along with the top four: *Ebony*, *Jet*, *Essence*, and *Black Enterprise*, and have enjoyed some gains in 2010.

- *Jones Magazine:* The mission of *Jones* is to serve as the premier shopping and lifestyle resource for multicultural women. Launched in 2005, it increased its circulation in 2010 because it expanded from a regional publication based in Houston to a nationally distributed magazine.

- *Uptown Magazine:* Describes itself as "the only luxury lifestyle publication for affluent African Americans." *Uptown* is distributed in several key urban markets including, Washington, D.C., Chicago, Atlanta, New York City, Charlotte, Detroit, and Philadelphia and enjoyed a 37 percent increase in circulation in 2010. It doesn't hurt that celebrity Star Jones, formerly of *The View* and *Celebrity Apprentice*, is the editor-at-large. *Uptown*'s total circulation remains smaller than the other four African-American oriented magazines. Still, its features, local content and unique events (i.e., partnership with BMW to honor outstanding African-American leaders during the Kentucky Derby) and overall success in 2010 spurred the magazine to increase its publication schedule from six to eight issues per year in 2011. What's also interesting about *Uptown*'s success is that it defies perceptions that younger Blacks don't want racially focused magazines.

As with general market publications, many Black magazines have also invested more in technology, online platforms, mobile apps and national events to engage their audiences and maintain brand relevance. Here's what some of major players and popular titles have been up to:

Ebony and Jet

In September 2009, I wrote on *Advertising Age*'s The Big Tent multicultural blog about the struggles and successes of *Ebony* magazine. Since at least 2006, chairman and CEO of Johnson Publishing, Linda Johnson-Rice has worked tirelessly to rebrand both *Ebony* and *Jet* and expand and balance their predominately older readers with a younger audience.

Over the years Johnson-Rice has engaged first class talent to revamp the publication, including *Ebony*'s former interim editor and master creative director, Harriet Cole, who helped create *Ebony*'s new look, and Desireé Rogers, former White House Social Secretary, as its CEO. Former Time Inc. managing editor for *Teen People*, Amy DuBois Barnett, replaced Cole as *Ebony*'s editor-in-chief.

And in May 2009, Mira Lowe was named editor-in-chief of *Jet*. Lowe, the former managing editor, oversees all aspects of the magazine's editorial content, staffing and evolving direction on both print and digital platforms and launched a makeover of the weekly's look.

Apparently Johnson-Rice's hard work is paying off. In 2011, as *Ebony* and *Jet* turned 65, they looked and read younger than their years. *Ebony* is striking. It is bold, beautifully designed, hip, contemporary and edgier than issues from previous years. The November 2011 cover featured actress Nia Long—most noted for her roles in *Boyz n the Hood, Love Jones,* and *Soul Food,* seven months pregnant and (tastefully) nude (think: Demi Moore, *Vanity Fair,* August 1991).

Jet's old rules are the new rules. In addition to an updated cover and graphics, the magazine is smartly holding on to its tiny size and a nice balance of features that work: news, important community information, Black stats, gossip, entertainment and the girl-next-door, swimsuit-posed, Beauty of the Week.

These improvements have helped *Ebony* and *Jet* hold their own in a very volatile print environment. As of this writing *Ebony* and *Jet* report readership at 12 million and 9.7 million respectively. The overhauled website Ebony.com (formerly EbonyJet.com) currently welcomes 400,000+ unique visitors monthly and over 2 million monthly page views.

By understanding the importance of engaging audiences across multiple platforms, *Ebony* and *Jet* have partnered with BET, TV One, YouTube, Code Black Entertainment (producers and distributors of programs for television broadcast and syndication) and the Gospel Music Channel to offer clients more solutions and connections to a broader Black audience.

Black Enterprise

Black Enterprise defines itself as more than a magazine, but rather a total media firm with a singular mission: "We will educate and empower our audience to become full participants in wealth creation within the global economy." In doing so, for the last several years, *BE* has broadened its scope to include a strong online presence with videos, blogs, and content that features individuals, as well as business success stories. Importantly, *BE*'s events fulfill their mission and also physically bring clients and consumers together. Over the years, its Golf and Tennis Challenge, Entrepreneurs Conference, and its Women of Power Summit has attracted thousands of business-minded, goal-setting Black Americans who are willing to do what it takes to empower themselves and their community. The ability to attend these events and interact with this audience face-to-face has helped clients better understand their target. Moreover, the number of ad pages sold in Black Enterprise increased 12 percent in 2010.[7]

BE also connects with its audience via its weekly television shows. Aired in 145 markets, *The Black Enterprise Business Report* is a half-hour show that focuses on wealth building. *Our World* covers hot topics via exclusive interviews with headline personalities from the worlds of business, politics, and entertainment.

Essence

From the beginning *Essence* magazine recognized that African-American women had a unique viewpoint and style. Showing confidence in the opinions and decisions of its audience *Essence* presented expertise from authorities on beauty, style, health and more that helped propel readers to a more informed and sophisticated plane.

What has changed throughout the years is the scope of *Essence's* content. Beauty, fashion and health are still its core, but consumer data, travel and tourism facts and financial reporting have been added to the basics. Still taking the lead, the presence of *Essence* in the electronic community is critical too.

Its ezine connects it to a younger, upwardly mobile, technically aware urban woman. Recently added to the web array is an iPhone/iPad application that presents over 300 hairstyles users may try on an avatar or a downloaded photo of themselves. This easy-to-use, entertaining app will be periodically updated, and is just another example of *Essence's* intention to keep African-American women in the know and in style.

Essence.com touts its site as the number one destination for African-American women and therefore declares its authority on Black beauty and hair. The site welcomes more than one million visitors per month, who are on average, 39 years old and earn $47,500 per year. *Essence* Mobile reaches 544,000 users each month—an increase of 96 percent from January 2010, and its social media properties reach 125,000 users with 70,000 Facebook "Likes." It also has 55,000 Twitter followers with dozens of new users added each day.

Separately, the *Essence* family celebrated with an estimated 420,000 people at its 2011 Essence Music Festival, the largest event celebrating African-American culture and music in the United States. Attendance in 2011 was up by 20,000 over 2010.

Heart and Soul

Giving your heart and soul means using everything you've got. That's the philosophy of the magazine with that name. *Heart and Soul* deals with the total wellness of the African-American woman via her heart, her health, and fiscal and mental well-being—the entire package. Relationships with spouses, families and friends are explored, and readers can find essential advice and information. Every aspect of the publication is geared to creating a reader who is "healthy, wealthy and wise."

The *Heart and Soul* ezine connects readers to podcasts that highlight topics and products that educate and entertain, presenting the latest in merchandise and methods to increase holistically healthy living. Sweepstakes offer prizes that correspond to the magazine's monthly theme. The publication's bimonthly readership is 300,000 with a total audience of more than 1.5 million. The weekly electronic newsletter offers updates on these subjects to over 10,000 subscribers.

Sophisticate's Black Hair

Founded in May 1984, *Sophisticate's Black Hair* magazine is recognized by the American Health and Beauty Aids Institute—the association of Black hair-care product manufacturers—as the bestselling Black beauty magazine worldwide. Its aim is to provide women (and men) of color with the most current and popular styles and products for the African-American consumer. The magazine features an A-list celebrity on its cover, interviews about celebrity hair, beauty tips, and over 1,000 photographs of everyday, girl-next-door women modeling their coiffed styles. *Sophisticate's* takes the time to retouch these photos of real people that are submitted by local beauty and barber salons all over the country. It provides a nice "shout out" to them and keeps them and their customers loyal to the publication.

Sophisticate's is also capitalizing on the booming natural hair movement and has included a pullout section for braids and natural hair styles and an at-home guide to help readers duplicate featured hair styles. Beauty professionals rely on the "Salon Talk" column to learn about new products and trends in the market. The online magazine adds reader polls and surveys to this, and the magazine is on Facebook and Twitter.

XXL

XXL, the top selling ABC-audited music publication on newsstands worldwide, is the premier Hip-Hop media brand. *XXL* sets the standard in rap music journalism with the best writers and photographers in the industry, and chronicles all that's relevant in Hip-Hop culture. It attracts African Americans (67%), Caucasian/White (18%), Hispanic/ Latino (19%). The print version remains an industry frontrunner and is complemented by a popular website and iPhone app. The web magazine adds daily news updates, blogs and social media links.[8]

Upscale

In 1989 when Bernard Bronner of hair-care products fame launched *Upscale* magazine, it was carried on 35,000 newsstands nationally. Today its circulation is over 250,000. *Upscale* provides a forum for African Americans seeking news and exposure to what is stylish and smart in beauty, fashion, health and fitness, travel, and entertainment. For many readers *Upscale* represents a first look at what is tasteful and discriminating in and for the Black community for those who have reached (or aspire to reach) the next level. *Upscale* can be found on Facebook, Twitter, YouTube and it has a Flickr photostream.

TrueStar Magazine

TrueStar Magazine is a free publication created and produced by teens. It's a small local magazine, yet through paid after-school apprenticeship programs, teens learn to develop, write and edit content, produce layouts, sell advertisements, execute events, and market the publication. The magazine's editorial mission is to inform, entertain, educate and serve as the voice of urban youth in which they address everyday issues through life experiences and critical thinking. The student staff comes from sixteen Chicago high schools and includes Black, Hispanic, and Caucasian students. They are taught graphic design, marketing, journalism, web blogging, and editorial management. Other projects of the TrueStar Foundation include a blog and a radio station.

African American/Black Magazine Engagement

While some of the top experiences that drive readership for both African-American and general-market magazine readers are the same, many are not. The experiences that are different between the two groups and which are more important to Black readers than mainstream readers are:

• Building relationships
• Emotional relevance
• Visual appeal

Top Reasons to Advertise in Magazines

The reasons marketers advertise in general-market magazines are the same for advertising in Black magazines. According to magazine.org:

• Magazine audiences are expanding across platforms: The number of magazine websites and mobile apps is increasing, e-readers are projected to grow rapidly—and consumers want to see magazine content on them.

• Magazine advertising gets consumers to act.

• Magazines improve advertising ROI.

• Magazines contribute most throughout the purchase funnel.

• Magazines build buzz. They complement the web in reaching social networkers, whom marketers increasingly favor to generate word-of-mouth.

• Magazines prompt mobile action taking.

• Magazine advertising is valuable content.

• Magazines supply credibility: Multiple sources show that consumers trust ads in magazines.

• Magazines deliver reach.

• Most people in a magazine's audience read their copy within the first three days after receiving or buying it.

Television

African Americans watch more television than any other group. The average African-American household has four or more televisions, and spends an average of 432 mintues (about 7.25 hours)—or 213 hours per month—watching them. This amounts to about 40 percent more viewing time than the rest of the population.[9]

Black cable network television is a road filled with vision and hope in addition to achievement. Cable channels with mass Black audiences like BET, TV One, and The Africa Channel are valuable to advertisers as well as their audiences. They provide a medium and relevant programming that appeals to large numbers of Black Americans that can facilitate connections between these audiences and advertisers. Here's a snapshot of what broadcasters have been doing to remain relevant and connected to Black audiences.

BET

The leopard can change his spots. In an effort to improve its image and standing from a network that continues to be the target of criticism and protests for broadcasting videos and programs that promote stereotypes, BET returns to being one that truly inspires and informs the community it aims to serve and demonstrates that African Americans rally around culturally relevant programming and content.

Who better than Beverly Bond? The former Wilhelmina model and DJ is well suited to champion a movement for high self-esteem and value among Black girls aged 12 to 17. Bond founded Black Girls Rock! Inc., a non-profit mentoring organization, to empower girls as well as encourage a dialogue about the way women of color are portrayed in the media. Programs include creative writing workshops, college campus tours, mentoring programs, empowerment circles, a book club, and more. All of these efforts are showcased on a celebrity-rich awards show where exemplary women who embody the mission of the organization in their lives and work are honored from the worlds of business, politics, entertainment, sports, and community service.

In 2010 Ed Gordon, the award-winning journalist most noted for infamous interviews with O.J. Simpson, Trent Lott, and R. Kelly returned (after two previous stints at BET) to the network to host news programs and specials.

In response to Black consumers' requests for programming that speaks to Black family values and Black romantic love—two powerful connectors in the Black community—BET launched two scripted programs to address their needs: *Let's Stay Together* is a romantic comedy that highlights the modern relationships of five young, professional African Americans. The show is entering its second season with an average of nearly 3 million viewers since its launch in January 2011.

Malcolm-Jamal Warner from *The Cosby Show* and Tracee Ellis Ross from *Girlfriends* helped attract 3.3 million viewers during the debut of their show *Reed Between the Lines.* The sitcom showcases positive images of a Black family of five and particularly the affectionate husband and wife who are in love.[10]

January 11, 2011, marked a monumental day in BET history as the debut of *The Game* brought in 7.7 million viewers (equal to *The Oprah Winfrey Show* in its heyday). According to Matthew Barnhill, executive vice president of market research for BET, 80 percent of those viewers were Black. *The Game* sitcom stars Tia Mowry-Hardrict (*Sister, Sister*) as Melanie Barnett, a young woman who is thrust into the world of professional football when her boyfriend becomes a wide receiver for the San Diego Sabers.

It was originally broadcast on the CW network and cancelled after only 64 episodes. BET picked up the show after a few weeks of successful re-runs on its network.

Finally, BET Networks has begun pro-social initiatives that help raise awareness about AIDS and obesity and shed light on the legendary contributions African Americans have made to this world. These programs include Touch BET, Rap-It-Up, BE HEARD, the BET Foundation, and A Healthy BET.

The issue is not whether every TV show needs some perfect, artificial racial balance. It's whether TV overall, treats White as the default setting for stories that call for characters of mostly one race—family comedies, for instance. . . .

The Game's *ratings suggest it's simply good business to invest in shows about people TV has ignored.*[11]

—James Poniewozik

TV ONE

With a leadership team that has many years industry experience including new CEO, Wonya Lucas, TV One continues to be a vital media outlet for Black audiences. Cable network buzz is that Lucas is poised to take the network to the next level. Says Lucas, "It's an incredible opportunity to lead TV One, which in just a few years has become such a success story. I am also personally passionate about TV One's mission to provide high quality entertainment and information to the African-American audience that authentically reflects our lives, history and culture."

Over the years, TV One has listened to its viewers. *Unsung,* the NAACP Image Award–winning music biography series, and favorites including *Life After,* a "where-are-they-now?" look at actors and artists, help TV One generate increased audiences and ad revenue. *Washington Watch,* the public affairs interview program with Roland Martin, draws favorable audience numbers. The launch of TV One's first original scripted series, *Love That Girl,* a comedy starring Tatyana Ali, and the return of the successful reality program, *Lisa Raye: The Real McCoy* are just part of the 25 percent increase in original programming in 2011.

Repeat airings of shows starring Black performers add to programming that make the network compelling to African-American television viewers. TV One also offers exclusive special programming of events significant to the Black community such as the MLK Memorial dedication and the Essence Music Festival. Keith Bowen, TV One chief revenue officer, stated, "We will continue our efforts not only to sell the value of TV One but also the value of the African-American consumer."

The Africa Channel

The welcoming message on The Africa Channel's website boasts about its high quality, award-winning programming and rightfully so.

Its mission is to expose and "demystify" modern African life for American viewers. It does this by showcasing well-written and well-produced English language programming that includes news, documentaries, music, biographies, soap operas, current business analyses, and cultural and historical programs. I recall one story from *Africa Journal* that featured Rwandan school children using computers, the first generation after the 1994 Rwandan genocide. At another time while watching *Africa Music*, I grooved to music videos of authentic versus glamorized scenes of their R&B superstars.

The stories are indeed amazing as viewers are drawn into an almost *National Geographic* production style of African music, art, successes, challenges, and of course, Africa's beautiful landscape.

Radio

Marketers looking to connect with Black consumers might want to tune in to radio. "Ethnic formatted stations reach millions of listeners every day," says Alton Adams, Executive vice president and chief marketing officer of Arbitron Inc. "[Arbitron's] studies show the strength of radio as a media companion to ethnic consumers. Radio's relationship with ethnic listeners has been consistent over time; year over year, more than 90 percent of Black and Hispanic listeners tune in to radio for news, culture and sounds of the community."[12]

Radio isn't a dead medium in the Black community. But that's not to say everyone is in agreement about the relevancy of radio.

Marketers and media professionals struggle to make sense of the evolving trend in radio listeners in the Black community. It is easy to see how there can be such confusion when we compare the 2006 Bedroom Study findings to Arbitron's 2011 Black Radio Today Study results.

The 2006 Bedroom Study tells us that radios have disappeared from the bedrooms of many, especially the younger generation and implies that radio listening is declining. However that is not the full story according to Jay Stevens, VP programming content for Radio One.

"It's not a decline in listenership. Ninety-four percent of Americans listen to the radio every week," says Stevens. He balks at the Bedroom Study's implications, agrees with Arbitron's findings, and provides clarity between the two findings.

"People still listen to the radio because they love the radio. What we're finding is a decline in the amount of time they're spending with radio because of other media options that are available to them, We're flooded with other choices like YouTube, iPod, or apps—now the list is 30 items long of places that you can go to get video/audio entertainment," says Stevens.

"African Americans have a very different relationship with radio versus general market listeners," adds Amy Vokes, VP and director of research for Radio One.

Vokes goes on to support this statement by sharing a key insight from one of the numerous research studies that she oversees adding, "We conducted research among our listeners at one of our stations which has primarily a female target—both Black and White. We were blown away to learn that for White females, it's all about the music. But for Black women, it's all about the station being a part of their lives, their community. They look forward to listening to the personality. They trust the personality. They trust the radio station."

Vokes's statement provides a valuable insight for marketers. In the Black community, "appointment radio" is very real and relevant to the millions who tune in daily to three popular syndicated radio hosts: Steve Harvey, Tom Joyner, and Doug Banks. Harvey, Joyner, and Banks most likely capture the majority of Urban Adult Contemporary, Urban Contemporary, and Rhythmic Contemporary listeners, which explains why these categories continue to rise. (*See* Black America *Is* Listening, *page*

169) These personalities have generous souls and use their celebrity to give back to the Black community.

Top Three Syndicated Black Radio Shows Highlight the Value of "Appointment" Radio

Tom Joyner	Steve Harvey	Doug Banks
Reaches 8 million in over 105 markets	Reaches 7 million listeners in over 64 markets	Reaches 3.2 million listeners in 42 markets
Culture, Health, Family and community are Joyner's passion points. Connects with millions online via blackamerica web.com, a news and entertainment site. Connects with tens of thousands at sponsored events and initiatives including: • Take a Loved One to the Doctor • Real Fathers, Real Men • Tom Joyner Cruise benefiting the TJ Foundation for HBCUs	Bigger than life with his listeners, 18-34 and 25-54; His first book *Act Like A Lady, Think Like A Man*, released on January 27, 2009, became the #1 *New York Times* best-selling advice book! Steve Harvey Foundation helps young men, become productive men who are balanced emotionally, politically and economically. Hoodie Awards honors community businesses and leaders in 12 categories. Several celebrities join Harvey and honorees.	Banks and popular co-hosts DeDe McGuire and comedian Rudy Bush use Facebook, Twitter, and the show's website to connect with listeners. Honored in November 2005 at the Annual Living Legends Foundation Gala for his outstanding achievements and contributions as a trailblazer in the radio entertainment community. The Doug Banks Literacy & Scholarship Initiative supports the development of a fully-literate American population by raising awareness about illiteracy and getting the private sector actively involved in supporting literacy across the country.

In addition to Urban, and R&B, inspirational music is another category that is popular with African Americans. Although religion is vital—a big deal to many Black Americans because it is viewed as the cornerstone for survival, today spirituality is bigger.

In an attempt to be politically correct about programs that they buy, many advertisers shy away from "Religious" formats. "Religious" is a standard format description used by the radio industry, the music played on Black Religious stations is not about religion *per se*, it's about spirituality and the inspiration that the music provides.

According to Arbitron, Gospel enjoyed the longest Time Spent Listening rates of all formats targeting Black listeners, especially younger ones. It was number 2 only to Urban Adult Contemporary among those aged 12 to 24 and in various adult demographics. Time Spent Listening decreased just 15 minutes per week overall, but gained among 18 to 34 year olds—the only music format to do so. Additionally, "Religious" saw 30-minute gains among those 12 to 24 and a full hour uptick with adults 18 to 34.[13]

In his bestselling book, *Conversations with God,* Neal Donald Walsch defines *religion* as "someone else's experience" and *spirituality* as "your own experience."

There is a high level of engagement from listeners for inspirational messages. Study after study reveals that in spite of their particular hardships, African Americans are more optimistic about their futures than all other segments. For many African Americans, spirituality is about doing the "right thing," being positive, hopeful, encouraged, and marketers who understand this and engage African Americans through inspirational programming win.

Walsch's definitions of religion and spirituality fit well with how Radio One and American Urban Networks (AURN) market their inspirational radio programming. AURN, the only African American–owned network radio company in the United States, fully embraces the inspirational terminology and programming. They have a partnership with the Sheridan Gospel Network (SGN), which enables them to integrate marketing ideas across a 24-hour syndicated inspirational programming network.

As a result of client-sponsored programs like *The Yolanda Adams Morning Show,* Radio One has seen success by positioning the show as inspirational versus religious. "Listeners feel that clients are good people that they could trust because they have similar values," says Jay Stevens, senior VP of programming content for Radio One. "We're going into year three with Lowe's as being probably the largest sponsor of the

Yolanda Adams Show and their internal research tracking has shown growth among African Americans," he adds.

Black radio engages audiences via technology

"Black radio matters today because it's not just 'Black Radio' anymore. It exists on a number of platforms virtually everywhere the Black audience is. . . . it's a much more personal, intimate level when somebody can listen to their favorite radio station on a smart phone and they can instantly engage, react and participate in the conversation they're hearing through texting and other digital platforms."

—Dan Shelley, General Manager, Digital, Radio Division, Radio One

Dan Shelley said a mouthful, given Black Americans' propensity as early adapters of technology—they are more likely to own smartphones and cell phones with app-based, web-based operating systems. The creation and use of downloadable streaming apps as another means for engaging Black radio only *seems* obvious; in reality it's ground breaking. Being able to "take my world with me" is an idea whose time has come.

Most Americans embrace technology and the idea of "taking the world with me," but "taking my world with me" is particularly important to ethnic communities and underserved segments. Marketers must pay attention to the "my" in this phrase. It's personal and speaks to the two worlds in which Blacks and other minorities live.

Internet access for many African Americans is not on the computer. Due to several factors including availability and cost, internet access by African Americans has sidestepped the desktop and laptop for the cell phone. The cell phone, especially in homes with no broadband access, has become "their default gateway to the internet," says S. Craig Watkins, an associate professor at University of Texas at Austin.[16]

According to Pew Research, "African Americans and English-speaking Latinos continue to be among the most active users of the mobile web." In fact, 44 percent of African-American teens use their cell phones to access the internet vs. 35 percent and 21 percent of Latino and White teens respectively.

Thus, mobile devices are the new primary internet vehicle for many African Americans. Moreover, 33 percent of all African Americans own a Smartphone, and 44 percent of all new mobile phone purchases by this group are Smartphones.[14] "Hundreds of thousands of downloads happen within seconds and it's absolutely huge," says Barry Mayo, president of Radio for Radio One. "We want to be able to say to marketers, 'Here's an opportunity for you to effectively connect with this audience in a way that maybe you didn't think about."

> We've been at this for 30 years now, and we've built an intense relationship with our audience. When we got into the digital game, it allowed people to react to us, interact with us and engage us instantly via text messaging, through Facebook and Twitter and allowed them to comment on our stories and features that appear on our website . . . it's a way for them . . . not just to be a part of our audience, but to participate in what we do.
>
> —Barry Mayo, president of Radio, Radio One

Similar to Pandora, where listeners can create custom play-lists of their favorite songs by downloading them via the Pandora app, Clear Channel Communications offers listeners the opportunity to create their own "custom radio" via its newest product, iHeartRadio. Listeners create their own customized radio station based on their favorite songs, artists, or genres from over 750 stations. Not a Black concept, but Clear Channel, apparently aware of the Black mobile and digital phenomenon, has been heavily promoting these features on its Black radio stations. Additionally, BlackPlanetRadio.com allows users to create playlists from a library of more than 14.5 million songs to share with their social network communities.

Black Americans are not abandoning radio; they're discovering new ways to use mobile and digital to listen to the radio stations or channels that interest them. Marketers need to tune into the conversation that radio is having with Black America.

More than 87 percent of advertising and media executives say they will be moving a larger percentage of their content for mobile consumption over the next couple of years. Through mobility, Black content creators now have a way to bypass the gatekeepers of distribution and position culturally relevant content directly in front of the intended audience on one of the most personal items people carry with them all day long. Failure to adopt mobile means you aren't where your customers are.

—Michael Ferguson, CEO, OmniSource Events

Black America *Is* Listening

The following highlights from Arbitron's "2011 Black Radio Today" identify growth areas and segments associated with Black Radio listeners and substantiate the value of Black radio:

- **About 94% of Black consumers listened to radio every week.**Despite a growing number of media choices, radio boasted near-universal reach with Black consumers.

- **Listening by older Black men increased.** In recent years, a steadily higher percentage of men aged 35 or older have tuned in during weekday middays, afternoons, and evenings.

- **Urban Adult Contemporary continued as America's favorite format among Black listeners for the fifth straight year.** Urban AC has increased its share of listening every year since Spring 2005, and in Fall 2010 reached an all-time high—74% above the nearest format alternative.

- **Urban Contemporary and Rhythmic Contemporary Hit Radio's 35-to-54 audience composition rose.** Urban Contemporary was No. 2 to Urban Adult Contemporary with those aged 35-to-44, up from fifth last year. Its 35-to-54 composition rose from 29% in 2002 to 34% in Fall 2010. Rhythmic CHR's 35-to-54 audience segment climbed from less than 32% in Fall 2009 to 34% in Fall 2010.

- **Adult Contemporary's popularity grew.** AC drew 5.5% of all listening by Blacks, up from 5% in Fall 2009; that 5.5% is the largest share this format has delivered to date.

- **Among leading formats, radio's gender balance among Black listeners remained steady.**

- Away-from-home's proportion of Black radio listening rose.
- **Five formats registered new highs in out-of-home percentages: Urban Adult Contemporary (Urban AC), Urban Contemporary, Adult Contemporary and Soft Adult Contemporary (AC), Pop Contemporary Hit Radio (Pop CHR) and Rhythmic Contemporary Hit Radio (Rhythmic CHR).** Among the 10 formats measured year-to-year, radio listening somewhere other than at home rose from less than 54% in Fall 2009 to nearly 57% in Fall 2010.

―――

Social Media

The internet explosion and subsequent development of social media and internet platforms like YouTube, Facebook, Google and Mobile OS have created a massive change in media. It has also created a complicated challenge for media planners and buyers around how to maximize connections to targeted groups during a time where there are so many media choices.

Included in the social networks of Black Americans, both young and old, are platforms often created by and targeted to Black Americans. This contributes to an online world and powerful blogosphere in which topics relevant to African Americans get bandied about easily and en masse.

Traditional media are still very important, but the advent of social media provides marketers with another critical outlet for strengthening relationships with their constituents and consumers. This is a transitional time in marketing but there is currently a knowledge gap as to how to engage certain multicultural groups online.

New Digital Divide: The Internet Offers Distinct Experiences [*]

We still have a pretty segregated set of experiences . . . those often writing about Twitter for a mainstream audience also tend to reflect the networks that they see.

―Baratunde Thurston, web-editor, *The Onion*
and author, *How to Be Black*

As marketers continue to drop traditional ethnic media and scramble to create the "ultimate cross-cultural digital experience and platform," they should notice America's behavior on the web. Youth are everywhere on the web, but ethnic internet users, both younger and older, are "congregating in spaces where there are people like them, or where they feel comfortable bringing people like them," says Ebele Mora, a Millennial, and chief financial officer for TUV Mediaworks.

Most multicultural and LGBT groups seek places on the web beyond cross-cultural lifestyles in an effort to connect with others from their own culture or sexual orientation. Congregating provides the opportunity for these segments to engage in shared experiences related to their cultures, lifestyles, and music.

Importantly, given that society penalizes those who openly discuss racial issues, these spaces provide a refuge for honest conversations about subjects that affect their communities. One Black GenY Facebooker confessed that frequently, she temporarily blocks her White Facebook friends—and prays they don't notice—so that she can have open, honest discussions with her Black friends. When Representative Joe Wilson shouted "You lie!" to President Obama during the President's health-care speech, Black social media exploded when Black Twitterers and Facebookers sent numerous tweets, posted on walls, and flocked to Black platforms. Mainstream bloggers' hand-slap to Wilson was different from the Black community's comments and conversations about the "disrespectful" and "racist" Wilson. Subsequently, the Black web community surmised that society still doesn't get or respect Black America.

Thurston's comment above that called out mainstream web writers who have a limited view of ethnic group activity on the web is dead on. Mention Bossip, Jack & Jill Politics, KissMyBlackAds, theGrio, The Root, or DimeWars—popular sites that attract thousands of Black visitors—to these self-described trend watchers and wait for their reaction: speechless (and priceless).

There's a powerful Black digital and social networking world going on and many marketers and digital gurus don't have a clue. The added value that most of these Black platforms and social networking groups provide is a comfort level not experienced in some commercial mainstream platforms. They tend to deliver a FUBU–effect (For Us By Us) in that visitors feel safe to be "real" and have a closed conversation.

"In many ways, these platforms serve as virtual barbershops and beauty salons," said multicultural strategist Herb Kemp. Kemp also added: "Visitors are more likely to express what they really feel in these spaces and are less worried about offending others as in commercial spaces where there may be more diverse groups of people."

Arianna Huffington, co-founder of *The Huffington Post,* joined forces with AOL Black Voices to add an African-American section, and subsequently will follow with a Latino section. BET co-founder Sheila Johnson cited this move as significant given that "the African-American voice is falling off the radar screen [in the digital space]."

I don't think the Black voice is falling off the screen. In some cases, the digital space has become the new virtual real estate. "People tend to use the web in the way they live," says Ahmad Islam, co-founder and managing partner of Commonground Marketing, a full-service communications and digital strategy firm in Chicago. It makes sense given that America is still very segregated—Blacks, Whites, Asians, Latinos, and other groups are living, worshiping, and socializing primarily among themselves. Now, as Islam indicated, this practice has transferred to the web. Black fans of BET's *The Game* were galvanized around Black social networks and the Black blogosphere—not mainstream platforms—to catapult *The Game* into ratings history: 7.7 million viewers when the new season premiered on BET.

Marketers need to be careful about abandoning ethnic strategies in the digital space. The opportunity is to understand ethnic digital platforms and who, how, where, and when their consumers are showing up so that brands can better connect and engage them.

---

*A version of this segment appeared in *Advertising Age*'s The Big Tent

Blacks in Cyberspace

Like neighborhood newspapers, Black digital platforms can provide updates and summaries to a specific community in a variety of ways. Most of these platforms have common elements (links to Facebook and Twitter, blogs) but they are as diverse as *MAD* magazine and *Forbes*. Consider the following.

allhiphop.com The focus is the Hip-Hop society and its stars, fashions and music. Here rumors are posted and some are verified, or denied. A nuance here is an opportunity to get instant alerts on hot topics at your request.

Blackandmarriedwithkids.com A top independent marriage and parenting blog. Puts a positive spin on Black marriage, families, and parenting.

BlackYouthProject.com The Black Youth Project's website is a cyber-resource center for Black youth and all those who are committed to enriching the lives of Black youth.

Blackplanet.com The world's largest free African-American online community where Black women and men meet to chat, discuss, and engage on what matters to us.

Blackweb20.com The focus of Blackweb 2.0 is African-American interest and presence in the technology and new media. Items posted contain culturally relevant tech industry news and features on executives, entrepreneurs and those who influence it in the Black community.

Bossip.com This award-winning site (including Best Hip-Hop Blog in 2008 by VH1 Hip-Hop Honors; one of Yahoo! Top Ten Blogger's Roll, 2009) is the hottest and hippest for African-American pop culture and entertainment. It's candid, waggish, politically savvy, and exceptional.

Clutchmagazine.com The freshest, the flyest, the hottest online magazine for young women of color. Echo Boomers (aged 18–34) learn and create what's in and what's out on today's urban landscape. If it's important to an African-American female, you will see it on *Clutch*. Visitors to the site have increased in every quarter since it stated in April 2007.

Crunktastical.net Crunk (crazy drunk) and disorderly is the claim here—and this site seems to focus on delivering no-holds-barred, in-your-face news and information with much user feedback. Launched in 2004, this is one of the oldest African-American entertainment information sites.

HelloBeautiful.com An online lifestyle guide for Black women that encourages healthy and fabulous lifestyle choices.

Jack & Jill Politics (jackandjillpolitics.com) Since summer 2006 this award-winning political blog has influenced the national narrative on race and how African Americans react to the issues of the day. With guidelines and standards for participation, this site intends to provide a middle class African-American perspective on U.S. politics and to change the negative portrayal of Blacks in the media by engaging in knowledgeable social and political commentary within its cyber-community.

MediaTakeOut.com The bare-bones approach is what you find here. Photos and blurbs followed by comments from users is most of the site content, rather like talk radio online.

NecoleBitchie.com Most of the interviews and entries here are cattier with more of a negative slant. Necole states this is not a news site but her blog, composed of her attitudes and opinions, but clearly there is a niche in the market for this, too.

SingleMAMAhood.com The word "mama" is a flag, the connector to Black women in this website's name. Kelly Williams, a motivational speaker, educator, and single parent is the founder of this site. In addition to parenting tips, Williams encourages moms to not only respect themselves but the fathers of their children as well.

Vibe.com Represents over 25 sites and reaches over 19 million unique users per month. The new Vibe is the premier destination for urban music, entertainment, culture, and lifestyle.

Seventy-two percent of Black America is online and these Internet users are more active content producers online than other groups, according to emarketer. African-American online users are younger with a median age of 33 vs. 39 for the general population.

According to the Nielsen and National Newspaper Association's report, *The State of the African-American Consumer* (2011), African Americans are now 44 pecent more likely to take a class online, and 30% more likely to visit

Twitter. They download more movies via the internet than other ethnic communities. Additionally, during July 2011, there were 23.9 million active African-American internet users of which:

76% visited a social networking or blog site

54% visited a travel site

50% visited a mass merchandiser site

50% visited a current events and global news site

44% visited a health, fitness and nutrition site

39% visited a sports site

37% visited a coupons/rewards site

37% visited a broadcast media site

31% visited a financial information and news site

CASE STUDIES

Using Social Media Engagement to Heighten an African-American Health Cause: Power to End Stroke and Go Red for Women

By Kevin Walker CEO, CultureLab

Power To End Stroke

Background/Project description

Power To End Stroke (PTES) is an awareness initiative formed in 2006 by the American Heart Association and American Stroke Association to alert people to the devastation of cardiovascular disease, and stroke in particular. The aim is to get people to change their lifestyles to enhance their health and to stave off stroke. Although stroke impacts everyone, Blacks are at very high risk. Blacks have almost twice the risk of first-ever strokes compared to Whites. Blacks also have higher death rates from stroke compared to Whites. As a consequence of the exponentially greater impact of stroke on Blacks, PTES focuses most of its cause marketing on African Americans.

Objective

Our overarching objective was to increase PTES online registrants (Facebook likes) by 10 percent.

What we did: Build the audience . . . the earned way

As people are shifting more of their media consumption online and specifically through mobile, the social media platforms of Facebook, Twitter, and YouTube have become increasingly important. Traditional media is still important, but the advent of social media gives us another critical outlet for strengthening relationships with our constituents and consumers.

Building a targeted audience on Facebook

The ultimate goal was to promote ongoing two-way communication between PTES and its followers and to create an authentic voice educating on all things related to the prevention of cardiovascular disease.

For PTES, initially, we increased the audience simply by asking friends and supporters to "like" our Facebook page. We were also aggressive in building real connections with those who "liked" our page by daily responses to posts, engaging in conversation with passionate "posters," and scouring and posting powerful content related to the PTES subject matter. Through Facebook analytics, we learned that posting of video content and photographic content prompted people to interact more.

Email and Twitter

Email is another great vehicle we incorporated to help build our Facebook "likes."

Emailing your existing database and asking your existing database for likes (and Twitter follows) is one of the most powerful tools in building your social media following. On Twitter we concluded that the most effective way of building followers was by working aggressively to follow people in our respective space. If you "follow" people on Twitter you are apt to get a follow back.

Offline events help drive social media engagement

Social media offer a way to share information and create two-way communication. It means nothing if you have nothing to share or discuss. It is very important to have big events tied into your cause to serve as fodder for social media. Offline events are a great catalyst for social media engagement.

The Power to End Stroke Awards sparked our biggest increase in social media traffic. The awards show, and its ancillary events like the gospel tour leading up to the event, provided a platform for the cause. The mix of celebrities like Chrisette Michele, Terry Crews, and Anthony

Anderson (who hosted the show), and the PTES community created a powerful tool for content generation that was spread through Twitter and Facebook. It also served as a pep rally, of sorts, for the people in the trenches who worked day-to-day on behalf of the cause.

Results

Increased the number of Facebook likes by 19.8 percent. This was nearly double the stated goal.

We also increased post views (people who look at each post that is made on the Facebook page) and post feedback (people actually responding to each post with comments) compared with the same period in 2010. Post views increased by 281 percent and post feedback increased by 306 percent.

Our strategy and constant interaction via social media paid off.

Facebook Go Red For Women Campaign
Overview

On behalf of the American Heart Association, CultureLab created an African-American female-targeted campaign for its Go Red For Women (GRFW) initiative. The goal was to get African-American women to watch a 90-second, *Hands Only* CPR training video housed on GRFW's Facebook page.

Methodology

Ethnic targeting via Facebook requires a certain amount of cultural, lifestyle, and psychographic insight especially given that Facebook does not allow one to click a particular racial group. Since our charge was to target African-American women, we used behavioral data and online social profile information to help pinpoint our target. For example:

We knew that social status information such as membership in Black sororities like Delta Sigma Theta, Sigma Gamma Rho, or Alpha Kappa

Alpha are important "connectors" to help us learn about our target.

To pinpoint target profiles, we tracked preferences for classic movies like *Love Jones* (1997), and particular artists and entertainers who are favorites of Black women like Maxwell and Mary J Blige. We also used photography that reflected relevant images of Black women.

Results

Although click through rates (CTR) for social media platforms like Facebook are typically low, CultureLab helped generate a large number of targeted impressions (17.1 million) and an incremental 2,168 people clicked through to watch the CPR video within a two week period.

Grassroots Matter
SMSi Companies: The Grassroots Connector

Multicultural marketers who want to effectively reach and serve Black consumers often downplay the importance of working in the spaces provided by churches, beauty salons, barbershops, neighborhood venues, community based retailers including large and small chains, and the Black media, (traditional and social).

The SMSi Companies have specialized in large-scale national experiential programs for over 30 years.

Some examples of its grassroots programs include:

- The General Mills Feeding Dreams program, mentioned in an earlier chapter, highlighted Black community heroes as well as the important role of African-American women. SMSi forged a relationship with celebrity Susan L. Taylor, editor-in-chief emeritus for *Essence* magazine and founder of a non-profit, the National Cares Mentoring Movement (caresmentoring.org). Taylor's mentoring program for Black children has similarities with that of comedian and show host Steve Harvey who also has a mentoring program for young Black men, and who was similarly engaged.

- Working with Aetna Insurance, the SMSi companies managed appearances for Magic Johnson, an AIDS/HIV survivor and former NBA star. They created health and wellness events. Magic's mission—health literacy—was all about teaching Black consumers to read and understand the medical information they receive. For Aetna, SMSi created health fairs in Chicago, Los Angeles and Washington, D.C. and worked with AARP in Las Vegas, testing for diabetes, hypertension, and breast cancer, as well as hosting expert panels and speakers.

- For K&G Fashion Superstore, a new slogan, "Suit Up To Win: Body, Mind & Soul," was created, as well as a whole set of activities including free suit give-aways, church promotions, and a custom *Urban Call* magazine created around that theme. Black male celebrities who had suit lines at K&G headlined the *Urban Call–Men's Edition*, including actor Blair Underwood and comedian and show host Steve Harvey. Inside stories profiled men who are giving back to their communities. The publication was distributed in barbershops, in-store, and at community centers where Black men gather. Other articles on good grooming, job interviewing and positive thinking surrounded full-page ads featuring the suits, shirts, and shoes available at K&G. In the community, SMSi field ambassadors identified area "opinion leaders" and developed panels featuring Black men as role models and mentors who discussed topics such as finances and job hunting. The promotion was headlined as an "initiative for the empowerment of Black men."

These stories illustrate some of the ways to effectively and efficiently reach Black consumers. Using both traditional and new social media, SMSi's motto is "On-Site, On-Air, On-Line, On-Point and On-Shelf."

Notes

1. Emily Guskin, Paul Moore, and Amy Mitchell, *The State of the News Media 2011: African-American Media: Evolving in the New Era,* Pew Research Project for Excellence in Journalism.
2. Ibid., quotation by Danny Bakewell, who, in 2004, made history with the purchase of the *Los Angeles Sentinel,* one of the largest and most influential newspapers in the Western United States.
3. Cristina Fernandez-Pereda, "Florida Black Newspaper Seeks Partnerships to Survive Ethnic Media in the Recession," *New America Media,* August 20, 2009.
4. www.TriceEdneyWire.com.
5. Guskin, Moore, Mitchell, op. cit.; www.stateofthemedia.com.
6. Ibid.
7. Ibid.
8. Source: *XXL* Media Kit.
9. Nielsen and National Newspapers Association, *The State of the African-American Consumer,* September 2011.
10. Jonathan Landum Jr., "BET's *Reed* Offers Positive Images," www.shreveporttimes.com, October 21, 2011.
11. "Color Correction. Why Adjusting TV's Racial Balance Is Good for Business," *Time,* February 28, 2011, 66.
12. "Arbitron Looks at Ethnic Radio," *Target Market News,* February 25, 2010; Arbitron, *Black Radio Today 2009,* www.arbitron.com/downloads/black_radiotoday_09.pdf.
13. Arbitron, *Black Radio Today 2011,* www.arbitron.com/downloads/BlackRadio_Today2011.pdf.
14. Omar Gallaga, "Can Mobile Phones Narrow the Digital Divide," *Austin American-Statesman,* statesmen.com, July 4, 2010.
15. Nielsen and National Newspapers Association, "The State," op. cit.
16. James Briggs, "Four Tips to Boost Mobile Media Success," http://www.imediaconnection.com, August 5, 2008.

CHAPTER 14

Research Must Be Relevant

Marketers need to invest not only in relevant research but also to make sure that the people conducting the research have an understanding of the community being researched.

I don't know of any organization that has quantified the number of African-American professionals working in market research, but I imagine that those numbers are similar to, or worse than, employment figures for Black professionals in the advertising industry.

After presenting at a market research industry conference with other multicultural panelists, I took a little extra time to gather my things and check out before joining my fellow panelists for lunch in the main ballroom. As I passed through the ballroom's threshold, I was shocked at what I saw and what I didn't see. I hadn't been to one of these conferences in years, and here I was again panning a sea of White faces for brown ones. It was 2009, not 1969, and still there were not many brown faces in the room.

Seeing the not-so-diverse crowd reminded me how slow the market research industry has been in responding to three important opportunities:

1. Increase awareness of market research as a career among ethnic segments.
2. Recruit more people of color within all areas of the research industry.
3. Revamp research methodologies. In addition to new data

collection methods (web cams, video diaries, online research, bulletin boards etc.), foster relationships with anthropologists, identify and include grassroots methods that serve and connect with ethnic segments in a meaningful and relevant way.

Awareness seems to be such a big hurdle for the research industry to overcome. One big mistake that the industry makes is associating the word "underserved" exclusively with low-income and under-educated segments. The reality is that many educated African Americans, Latinos, and Asians are more likely than Whites to have little understanding of the market research industry, how it works and its processes. I can't tell you how many times my educated African-American friends have introduced my business profession and me incorrectly:

"This is my friend, Pepper. She has a _____
(*fill in the blank*: public relations, advertising, marketing or financial-planning) company."

It's this confusion that faces the marketing research industry. Attracting a diverse group of talented and qualified professionals should be a priority, given that minorities are not sure of the opportunities available to them in market research.

Calling All "Soldiers"

There is a group of people inside the industry that I like to call "soldiers" who are working to make the industry more reflective of the society.

Thank goodness for these "soldiers," who are not afraid to bring their whole selves to the table. In doing so, they challenge the status quo, raising questions or making suggestions relative to inclusivity. They encourage management to bring in more people of color. The results are positive.

Over the years, the number of inquiries from students of color about market research as a career option have increased only by a smidge, but have increased nonetheless. The "soldiers" can't do it alone, which is why The Hunter-Miller Group created the Ruth C. Hunter African-American Market Research Scholarship Fund to help increase awareness about market research to Black college students and encourage them to consider market research as a career option.

Missing the Cultural Nuances

When many companies plan their research, they believe that including two persons of color in a focus group, or including a small (and often unreliable) sample of ethnic consumers in a quantitative study among predominately White respondents, constitutes representation. I think not. In fact, cultural nuances are often missed in mixed-race qualitative studies. During mixed-race focus groups many Blacks, especially younger Blacks, are determined to steer clear of comments related to Black culture and lifestyle to make sure they are not viewed in a limited way, even though they may live, worship, and socialize with other Black people.

It is within those "cultural nuances" where the real gold nuggets of insights and truths lie. The challenge is to not only assemble a proper representation of a segment but also to have researchers who understand that these nuances exist and play a huge part in how each group will respond.

This is not a theoretical issue; it is a current problem that many don't realize is a problem. In quantitative studies where large samples are measured, many marketers purposely avoid asking "the race" question and tend to tabulate results without looking at segments by race. This is not done out of arrogance but from the misguided belief that they are being accepting of different people by not recognizing their differences. They are trying to practice the belief of a colorblind society, but they are missing one very important fact—people are different. Ignoring these differences is not the answer—acceptance is.

After observing several awesome research presentations from senior-level marketing thought leaders at the 2011 M2Moms Conference, I was surprised that none of the presenters segmented their findings by race—not one. These executives tended to believe that all moms could be engaged in the same way, or they were not aware of how different Black moms see themselves, and their life as a mom, from White moms.

If only they could take a page from David Morse's notebook.

Morse is the CEO of New American Dimensions, a full-service market research company serving African Americans, Latinos, Asians, youth, and LGBTs. As a White male charged with gathering research from Black males he realized that the standard focus group format would not yield the best results for the segment. So, he got creative.

He hired a Black male moderator and took cameras into a barbershop in the Black community to talk to Black men. The information obtained from the men was beyond rich! The men spoke openly and candidly about their lives and experiences as Black men living in America. The responses heard from these men would never have happened to this extent in a traditional focus group. These insights are documented in his 2007 video *Fade2Black* and can be viewed on YouTube.

Many marketers and market-research professionals stay within their comfort zones when planning and conducting market research. Intentionally or not, they overlook opportunities to identify touch points that could better connect them with ethnic segments.

Get Used to Being Uncomfortable

Marketers and market researchers need to get used to being uncomfortable. They also need to get creative. Traditional focus groups for all segments are becoming less effective. It's time to take the research to the target—seeking out traditional groups in non-traditional settings and venues that are more relevant to the lifestyles of their target audiences vs. what is more comfortable for them. In these settings, we will find deeper insights and have more impact. I think marketers will be surprised with what they discover.

Employing more people of color in the market research industry from the top down is critical as well. There's a strong need for more senior-level managers of color who bring a broader view of different populations so that relevant policies and practices can be put in place. Employing people of color will help to make handling grass roots efforts easier, like David Morse and his team did, because there will be people who are both knowledgeable and comfortable going into various communities.

We recently conducted a study with first-time Black moms, both younger and older, from lower and mid-high social economic status. We had a "heck of a time" trying to find research companies in major markets capable of recruiting the women for our study. Many didn't have a diverse staff, and therefore were not comfortable reaching out to the Black community. And those that were willing did not have a clue as to where to start. This should not be happening in America, in the 21st century!

There is value in partnering with companies that have ethnic expertise as well as those that understand technology, and have street teams that reach insulated communities like the Invisible Middles.

The industry needs more researchers like David Morse, who did not let his Whiteness stop him from meeting people where they are. The industry needs to get creative about how they conduct and gather market research.

CHAPTER 15

Blacks In Advertising Matter

Jim Glover's book, *Mad Man,* has a message for Madison Avenue.

With all the trappings of a suspense thriller, Jim Glover allows readers to walk in the shoes of the main character, Randall Joseph, a brilliant Black creative director who has come to the end of his rope after being bamboozled and ostracized by peers and colleagues in the advertising business.

Glover's James Patterson–like, short, cliffhanger-style chapters are the perfect pace for keeping up with the unraveling Joseph. Glover does such a nice job with character development that I began to care about Joseph. Disenchanted with the ad business, he becomes self-destructive, getting his revenge—using extortion and murder—from those who used and mistreated him. I was frustrated with him, angry with him, came to understand his pain and madness, and couldn't wait to see what happens next.

Importantly, Glover provides real insights into the not-so-fictional frustrations and sensitivities of Black ad people and their reactions to the attitudes, beliefs, and practices of Madison Avenue corporate adertising executives and their often (mis-) perceptions about people of color. Glover opens with the suicide of fictional character Kevin Townsend, which mirrors the real life story of a disillusioned and frustrated ad exec who jumped to his death from his high-rise condo some years ago.

Glover uses Joseph and his victims' conversations, to expose some very real and raw feelings about the advertising industry workplace environment. In one scene we hear Joseph, with gun in hand, complaining about exclusion, hierarchy, lack of access, and stolen ideas, while his frustrated victim points to Black executives who embrace victimization and therefore are viewed as ungrateful whiners.

What is particularly interesting are the ideas raised in the Afterword. Glover lays out the credentials of brilliant Black advertising executives like Harry Webber who created "national campaigns that became household words" such as the "I am stuck on Band-Aid" campaign, or Carol H. Williams who animated the Pillsbury Dough Boy and created the "Strong enough for a man, but made for a woman" campaign for Secret deodorant. He questions why, during this "level playing field" time of our life, are there no African Americans that head mainstream agencies in 2011 America?

This and other documented facts below, brought to light by the Madison Avenue Project (madisonavenueproject.com) underscore the realities of African-American ad executives' frustration:

- African Americans are under-hired in the advertising industry; African Americans should be 9.6 percent of the managers and professionals (based on national demographic data), but in 2008, only 5.3 percent of managers and professionals were African American.

- About 16 percent of large advertising firms employ no Black managers or professionals, a rate 60 percent higher than in the overall labor market.

- African-American employees are under-used in the advertising industry. Blacks are only 62 percent as likely as their White counterparts to work in the powerful "creative" and "client contact" functions in agencies.

- African-American advertising employees are underpaid in the advertising industry. Black managers and professionals are only one-tenth as likely as their White counterparts to earn $100,000 a year.

- African Americans are often excluded from "general market" agencies and find work only in agencies specializing in "ethnic markets."

Glover shows though fiction the feelings and truths of people who have been left out of the general-market world of advertising. Glover's protagonist, Joseph, makes us stop and wonder: What would happen if all the grievances that Black ad professionals have were ever truly brought to public attention? He reminds us that the possible result of "enough is enough" is never more imminent than it is today, as our industry still, after all these years, hasn't solved its problems with the time worn concept of simple "equal rights."

Preparing the Future of Advertising
The Marcus Graham Project

That name sounds familiar? It should. In the movie *Boomerang*, Eddie Murphy played Marcus Graham, a ladies' man, go-getting advertising executive. As his eyes opened to the real world, Marcus became a mentor for youth in the arts and media. Marcus Graham became the namesake for the project created by Lincoln Stephens and Jeffrey Tate. Brainstorming and daydreaming in their Chicago condo, the roommates decided they could and would create a change in the advertising and marketing industry as it existed at that time. "I started this effort because of the lack of diversity in the advertising and marketing spaces—really, media as a whole. There were too many instances where I saw those who didn't understand marketing to an African-American demographic doing so," explained Stephens.

Stephens and Tate envisioned a network of men employed in advertising and marketing joining to mentor the next generation of Black men seeking careers in those fields. In just four years the idea developed into the Marcus Graham Project. The board of founders contains 17 men and women who work in all areas of advertising and media volunteering to help ethnic minorities of both genders discover and choose this career path. Today the project consists of a national network of over 600 diverse professionals that focus on developing the next generation of thought leadership within the advertising, media, and marketing industries.

The Marcus Graham Project's mission is to identify, train, and mentor ethnically diverse young men and women in all aspects of the advertising, media, and marketing industrIES. Its vision is to provide long-term access to information, technology, financial, and human resources to strategically develop a viable pool of talent and leadership within those industries.

MGP has several programs. The iRC8 program began its fourth year in 2012. The 10-week summer boot camp brings together young minority leaders from across the country. iRC8 has garnered attention by introducing kids to what life is like in the media and advertising worlds. AT&T used the program participants to conduct a market research study for the company. The iRC8 team gets hands-on experience that will help them better understand these industries. Team research provided AT&T with valuable insights to help develop the next generation of telecommunications technology—value added on both sides of the equation.

In addition to iRC8, programs include *The Network,* an online database resource that provides a cyber-community and forum of over 500 members where both mature and emerging young professionals connect and forge a support system to assist in the guidance of career and leadership skills; *The Drum,* an online radio show where MGP members connect in real time with guest hosts who will provide helpful information and advice on industry topics and trends; and *Sound Bite,* the speaker's bureau and lunch & learn series.

"There are no more excuses to be made. The talent is out here and we're here to show people where to find them," said Stephens.

———

The Madison Avenue Initiative

Munson Steed, CEO of Steed Media Group, was appointed by Rev. Al Sharpton as director of the Madison Avenue Initiative (MAI), a program that addresses fairness in advertising under Sharpton's National Action Network (NAN). The numerous disparities in the creative marketplace (writers, art directors, film directors, PR, field production, and ad agencies) motivated Steed to lead the Initiative.

"Access is a major player in American society and one that often evades the Black community," says Steed.

MAI's philosophy has been to encourage corporations to step up their efforts to build working relationships with businesses of color. MAI has successfully pushed for corporations to make advertising purchases that approach the level of minority consumer patronage of their products in specific markets.[1]

Note

1. "Munson Steed, *Rolling Out* Publisher, Named Director of Madison Avenue Initiative," *Target Market News,* targetmarketnews.com, February 21, 2010.

CHAPTER 16

Why Black STILL Matters

It's Important to the Bottom Line

What do McDonald's, Procter & Gamble (P&G), and Coca-Cola (Coke) know that other companies don't know? That there's gold in the Black community!

For decades McDonald's, P&G, and Coke have made it a practice to understand and build relationships with ethnic communities. Why? Some might think these companies are simply trying to be good corporate citizens, but let's be honest—McDonald's, P&G, and Coke didn't get to be McDonald's, P&G, and Coke only by being good corporate citizens. They became what they are by recognizing how to grow their businesses.

Beginning with the Black community in prior years, McDonald's and P&G, in particular, not only saw the value of connecting with Black consumers, but they also recognized the influence that Black consumers had on mainstream segments. They found that a lot of the trends and tastes were originating within the Black community and later being adopted by mainstream segments.

Instead of waiting to "discover" the trend in the mainstream, they understood the advantage of recognizing it early on. So for years, during the development of mainstream marketing campaigns, the question to mainstream marketing teams was "What are the Black insights?" Given the dynamic growth of the Latino and Asian segments, the question has evolved to "What are the ethnic insights?" which means that insights from each segment—African American, Latino, and Asian—are explored, weighed, and included toward the development of mainstream campaigns.

Neil Golden, chief marketing officer for McDonald's USA and keynote speaker at the 2009 annual ANA (Association of National Advertisers) Conference, shared McDonald's practice of using ethnic insights to lead McDonald's overall marketing efforts.[1] By the way, leading with ethnic insights is not a new concept. For years, Carol H. Williams, president of Carol H. Williams Advertising, has been speaking to corporations about this practice calling it "selling to and selling through."

Golden explained that ethnic segments are leading lifestyle trends. He added that his team decided to "start with the ones who are setting the pace." It also makes sense given that 40 percent of McDonald's current U.S. business comes from Hispanic, Asian, and African-American markets.

Importantly, McDonald's overall philosophy toward multicultural marketing is that it is key to its business success. Multicultural marketing is not viewed as charity, nor is it used as a disingenuous expression during Black History Month. It is an important driver for maintaining current customers and attracting new business.

This approach to multicultural marketing reminds me of a story I heard about the Brooklyn Dodgers when they signed Jackie Robinson. It was a tough time back then for a Black ballplayer. But the Dodgers weren't trying to advance the cause of civil rights. They signed Robinson because they wanted to win. McDonald's and Procter & Gamble embrace multicultural marketing because like the Dodgers, they want to win!

And what a win McDonald's has had!

According to Golden, since 2002, U.S. business alone has grown by $10 billion or $750,000 per restaurant. That translates into an additional 1.8 billion customer visits each year or about 75,000 visits per restaurant. Restaurant cash flow grew 50 percent over the same period.

It's Important for Corporate Culture

My colleague and friend Dr. Robert Rodriguez, a professor at Kaplan University in Chicago, often speaks about the importance for marketers to move from "fix them to fix us." What Dr. Rodriguez has found is that instead of recognizing and leveraging the differences in people, many marketers try to have everyone measure up to the same standard. This starts internally and expands outward affecting everything the marketer attempts.

There is a lot that companies can learn from various ethnic groups but they first have to start with their own culture. It is hard to embrace consumers' differences when a marketer's own employees feel pressured to fit a mold. It took Sharon, a senior executive, years to admit publicly at her company that she was biracial, and years for Eric, another Black senior executive at a different company, to come out of the closet. Both tell me there were times during planning sessions when providing insights into their worlds were critical toward the development of ethnic planning. How many planning sessions had their companies held that didn't have the benefit of their insights and understanding because they felt a need to hide who they were? What insights were missed? What mistakes could have been avoided? How far ahead could their respective companies have been with their full participation?

Another young brand manager from a large consumer package goods company wants to work on ethnic marketing, but has a fear of being pigeon-holed, labeled, and devalued, because at her company ethnic marketing isn't valued and is even considered as a barrier to success.

"I'm interested in ethnic marketing because it's my culture, and I want to see where this company is really coming from. I'd like to use my personal experiences to help out, but if you're Black you can get stuck here (ethnic marketing). What am I suppose to do?"

What *is* she to do? More importantly, what are companies to do when they are not getting the best or most qualified employees working on their marketing efforts because they fear being "trapped?"

Earlier, I wrote how American corporate culture suggests that successful people of color, particularly those elevated to high-level positions, abandon their culture and heritage, and particularly for African Americans, their "Blackness." Think about how much we can learn from those who are different if they are allowed to bring their whole selves to the table.

- "My" becomes "We."
- Ideas become strategies for real and relevant connectors.
- Corporate culture becomes open, inviting, invigorated, and includes loyal, happy employees.

The success of any multicultural marketing, like any marketing effort, must have senior management buy-in along with the company's commitment to the plan. Senior managers must not only sanction multicultural marketing, they must be actively engaged and involved in the process.

Another practice of "fix us vs. fix them" is the inclusion of ethnic advertising agency partners in the marketing strategy discussions early and often, recognizing the agencies as full partners during the process.

"Partner" is the key word here; it should not be used frivolously or superficially.

Few ethnic agencies have the opportunity to sit down and collectively work on the multicultural strategy. They are not even given the opportunity to work on or share their thoughts on the mainstream advertising. Instead, ethnic marketers are given "assignments"—not "the account"—and are often asked to adapt the general-market strategy to ethnic audiences. There's that "trying to make everyone meet a standard" thing again.

Not only does this process alienate the ethnic advertising agency, it also sends an unspoken message to all involved as to what the perceived value of the ethnic marketing is to the marketer. On top of that, marketers often direct ethnic agencies to mirror the general market's efforts. This practice prevents the strategy from being relevant to the ethnic segment.

Additionally, budget cuts are now the norm for all of marketing. No segment is safe. However, in 2009 McDonald's made sure that spending supporting its marketing efforts represented the country's ethnic makeup, 15 percent for Hispanic marketing, 12 percent for African Americans, and 5 percent for Asians. This insured that each segment was adequately supported with the funds needed to make an impact.

For years, P&G has taken a different tack by identifying key brands with strong African-American ties, and from the combined budgets of those brands allocated a minimum of 13 percent to the Black consumer segment.

The bottom line: the key to success in Black marketing is not only having a presence in the corporation, but also being present in the community, internally and externally.

It's important for *American* culture and all ethnic groups, so that we as marketers can understand and tell their stories.

The face of business and how business is conducted is not changing. It has changed.

It's Important to Prepare for the World Stage

Technology has made this a world economy. Business is being conducted in places and with people many marketers never imagined they would be. Before companies can make a global impact, they need a strong base upon which to launch on the world stage. That's hard to do when marketers don't even understand their own culture.

Marketers must be willing to better understand the segments that make up the whole. Not fully understanding or appreciating subtle differences on the world stage can have a huge and devastating impact on the success of a company. Recovering from such mistakes can require massive amounts of time, money, and manpower, causing companies to fall even further behind.

It makes great business sense to develop this sensitivity at home before trying to practice it abroad. The Black community represents an opportunity for marketers to learn how to recognize, accept, and incorporate this sensitivity into their efforts. There are many lessons waiting to be learned. Consider how many marketers perceive moms in America: most moms are the same and they share the same issues. Believing that, marketers focus their efforts on moms' concerns for the health and welfare of their kids, and on mothers' need for some "me" time, and think that they are creating an appropriate message. Well, it's not as good as they think.

> **Reality check:** Seventy-three percent of all Black births are to single mothers. (I stopped dead in my tracks when I learned this.) Recognizing and understanding this, an in-tune marketer would realize that, while daunting for sure, this is also an opportunity. While single moms in general constantly fight against stigmas, many single Black moms struggle with "Black mom" stigmas and stereotypes.
>
> These mothers believe they are different from White mothers. They believe they get less support from the family of the baby's father than a single White mother. They also believe they are stereotyped as welfare queens and that they do not raise well-behaved children. This is an opportunity for advertisers to create a relationship with Black mothers, to tell their stories and make them feel important and relevant.
>
> Just because a Black mom feels different doesn't mean an advertiser can't make her feel special.

Recently a marketer asked me how much money I thought marketers were leaving on the table by not engaging the Black Audience?

"What percentage of $957 billion do you think they'd like?" I replied.

The interesting thing about writing a book like this is that I came into it knowing what I wanted to say. I've been working in research for many years, and I've seen the numbers and statistics, and yet even I've learned a couple of things.

First, the more I researched and worked on this book, the more I came to realize how critical it is for marketers (and society in general) to understand Black America—its culture, value, influence, and complexities, and to continue the conversation.

Surely, if marketers were working at an optimal rate to engage Black America, they would see better bottom lines, and hear from fewer African Americans who believe marketers "don't get them."

> *Understanding people certainly impacts your ability to communicate with others . . . If you can learn to understand people—how they think, what they feel, what inspires them, how they're likely to act and react in a given situation—then you can motivate and influence them in a positive way.*
>
> —John C. Maxwell, internationally recognized leadership expert, speaker, coach, and author of *The John Maxwell Daily Reader*

Second, writing this book also reminded me of the importance of taking the time to understand "the basics," which is the infrastructure for big ideas. I will be the first to admit that the ideas expressed here are not necessarily new, but they are powerful in their simplicity. Yet they go unnoticed or unheeded because many marketers fail to see the value in the simple insights. Before we can do the complicated, we need to master the simple.

Before marketers can garner the support and loyalty of the Black community, they must first:

- Understand the importance and impact of portraying Black men in a positive light, and the power of showing Black men as role models in the Black community.

- Recognize the growing power and influence of Black social networks and the Black blogosphere, and how and why engaging Blacks in cyberspace can have a profound positive impact on marketers' bottom lines.

- Realize how young, single, and accomplished childless Black women break the stereotypes about young Black women, and the benefit of looking beyond the stereotypes.

These "simple insights" are the pathways to bigger and richer ideas.

Everyday, this world of ours grows smaller and smaller, technology is creating a truly global business community and the key to succeeding in this changing world lies in learning to recognize and understand the different segments of this ever-expanding business community.

My goal with this book is to give you something that causes you to think differently, more broadly and thoughtfully about Black America. To help marketers see the potential that lives and breathes in better understanding the Black community.

Not only does **Black STILL Matter,** it matters more today than it ever has.

Note

1. Emily Bryson York, "Ethnic Insights Form Foundations of McDonald's Marketing," *Advertising Age,* November 6, 2009.

About the Author and Contributors

Pepper Miller founded The Hunter-Miller Group (HMG), a leading-edge market research and strategic planning firm. Since 1985, HMG has provided real insights that have helped Fortune 500 companies effectively and positively market their brands to Black Americans. Some of these corporate clients include: American Airlines, Allstate, General Motors, General Mills, GlaxoSmithKline, Ford Motor Company, Johnson & Johnson, PepsiCo, Procter & Gamble, Toyota, and the Chicago Symphony Orchestra.

Pepper co-authored with Herb Kemp, *What's Black About It? Insights to Increase Your Share of a Changing African-American Market,* which many consider to be the most important book of insights about African-American cultural marketing. She served as a research consultant for the largest study about African Americans to date; the Black America Today segmentation study—commissioned by Radio One and conducted by Yankelovich.

In July 2007, Pepper received the *Target Market News* MAAX Award for Research Executive of the Year.

Pepper also established the Ruth C. Hunter Market Research Scholarship Fund to increase market research awareness among Black American students and encourage them to consider market research as a career option.

Pepper is a founding blogger for *Advertising Age*'s The Big Tent multicultural blog and is a frequent guest speaker for major corporations and at marketing conferences.

Howard Buford is president & CEO of Prime Access, which he founded in 1990 as a full-service advertising agency specializing in creating marketing communications targeted to African-American, Hispanic, and gay consumers. Prior to that, he was vice president/worldwide category supervisor at Young & Rubicam New York. He received a Clio award for his advertising work with AT&T.

Howard began his marketing career in packaged goods brand management at Procter & Gamble. He is an alumnus of Harvard College, where he graduated *magna cum laude* with an A.B. degree in linguistics, psychology and social relations. Howard also attended Harvard Business School, where he earned an MBA degree.

In 2008, Prime Access received the "Best African American Advertising of the Year" award from the prestigious Association of National Advertisers for *pro bono* advertising produced for the Partnership for a Drug-Free America and the White House's National Youth Anti-Drug Media Campaign. Prior to that, the company won the ANA's award for best GLBT advertising of the year for work produced for Volvo. Most recently, Prime Access won the pharmaceutical industry's PhAME Award for best multicultural pharma advertising for two consecutive years.

Howard has lived in both Amsterdam and Rio de Janeiro. Through his interest in foreign languages and cultures, Howard has become proficient in French and German, and traveled to some 40 countries throughout Europe, South American, Asia and Africa.

J.P. James, a published and award-winning advertising executive, has helped marketers win within many different business categories over the last 17 years at some of the top agencies in the business.

He is presently a senior partner of engagement planning at GroupM's MEC. In this role, he leverages consumer insights into media planning and activations for AT&T. He also is presently the director of account planning at boutique agency Spike DDB—the agency owned by noted filmmaker, Spike Lee. Prior to Spike DDB, J.P. was a brand planning director for GlobalHue's New York office, leading African-American strategy. In his spare time, J.P. is an adjunct professor at New York University where he teaches courses in multicultural marketing, and at Hunter College where he teaches public relations.

Sarah Lattimer is president and CEO of Lattimer Communications, a full-service advertising and public relations agency in Atlanta, Georgia, with a focus on the African-American, particularly female and Latino, segments.

Throughout her career as a marketing, advertising, and sales professional, Sarah has spearheaded highly successful, integrated, multicultural marketing campaigns. Under her guidance, Lattimer Communications recently completed a national, ground-breaking study, *A Profile of Today's*

Black Woman that received national attention from *The Wall Street Journal,* *Target Market News* and *Yahoo Finance,* among others.

A native New Yorker, Sarah began her career at McCann-Erickson and has worked at J. Walter Thompson, N.W. Ayer and Lockhart & Pettus where she was vice president/management supervisor overseeing the Dark and Lovely hair-care business. She also served as vice president of Chase Manhattan Bank where she was responsible for the sales and marketing efforts of the branch system.

The Atlanta Business League named Sarah one of the 100 Most Influential African-American Women in Atlanta. *Rolling Out* magazine also named her one of the Top 25 Most Influential Women in Atlanta.

Reginald Osborne is senior vice president, multicultural marketing, for Arnold Worldwide, responsible for helping to develop its multicultural marketing function. He currently supports the McDonald's CO-OP in Washington, D.C., and Baltimore by developing brand and retail promotions targeting African-American and Hispanic consumers. Prior to joining Arnold, Reginald was on the client side at Novartis Pharmaceuticals, where he was co-architect of the Multicultural Center of Excellence and developed multicultural marketing initiatives to support the cardiovascular brands. Before Novartis, Reginald was a senior account director at Spike DDB where he discovered his passion for multicultural marketing. While at Spike DDB, Reginald developed marketing programs targeting African-American consumers for Foxwoods, State Farm, Jaguar, Land Rover, Frito-Lay, and Exxon/Mobil.

After earning an MBA from Clark Atlanta University, Reginald began his marketing career in brand management at Nabisco Foods

Group. He next moved to the agency side joining Wunderman Cato Johnson where he gained experience in relationship marketing promotions on campaigns for AT&T wireless. From Wunderman, Reginald then moved to Bates Advertising and supported the T. Rowe Price and Johnson & Johnson accounts.

Reginald is a native of Savannah, Georgia, and a graduate of Savannah State University where he earned a BA in Business Management. Reginald currently resides in Maplewood, New Jersey.

Kevin Walker founded CultureLab in 2006 and has built a firm based on his ability to predict cultural trends and how they impact consumer behavior. He describes himself as "an entrepreneur, music geek, cultural snob, marketer, researcher, lecturer, and wanna be DJ who runs a strategic marketing services agency."

CultureLab is also about social media outreach, research storytelling, brand storytelling, and the production of video content for social media. Its clients include American Heart Association, Saatchi NY, General Mills, InTouch Credit Union, Nokia Latin America, SYAM Companies, and Dr Pepper Snapple Group. Says Walker, "My work is one of the things that defines me, so I don't take it lightly."

Index

100 Black Men of America, 111
2009 IMAGES USA Millennials Study, The, 16
2010 Census, 88, 90
2011 Black Radio Today Study, 162, 169–170
2011 M2Moms conference, 184

A Girl Like Me (documentary), 43
A Profile of Today's Black Woman (study), 122
Abandoned Minority, 140
Abbott Sengstacke, Robert, 151
Abernathy, Will, 110
About Face, (book), 59
Abyssinian Baptist Church, 67
acculturation, 86
Adams, Alton, 163
Adams, Paa Kwesi, 121
Advertising Age, xi, xiii, 7, 118, 154
advertising, 6, xvii, 13, 16, 27–28, 35, 50, 59,
  68, 86, 102, 113, 124, 130, 135–136, 146–147,
  159, 168, 187–191, 195
Aetna Insurance, 180
affluent Blacks, 18, 23–25
African American
  filter, 29–31
  portrayals in media, 15, 36–38, 60, 104,
  109
African American Financial Experience, The
  (report), 26
African Americans Revealed (study), 147
African immigrants, 82–83, 93
African-American Literature Book Club, 54
African-American Travel Conference, 70
Afro Latino, 83–86
Akinola, Oluwasegun (blogger), 82

Ali, Jamal, 131
Ali, Tatyana, 162
American Airlines, 70
American Health and Beauty Aids Institute,
  157
American Urban Networks, 166
Anderson, John and Maggie, 117–118
AOL Black Voices, 172
Arbitral, Inc., 163–165, 169
Arnold, Tim, 110
aspirational, 24, 114
Association of National Advertisers, 193
automotive brands, 56–65

Baarda, Brent, 19
Baby Boomers, 10, 12, 26, 115–121, 145
Bakewell, Danny Sr., 152
Bakula, Scott, 38
Ballentine, Warren, 117
banking, 25–26, 53
Banks, Doug, 117
Barker, Justin, 16
Barnett, Amy DuBois, 154
Barnhill, Matthew, 161
Basiden, Michael, 117
Basir, Qasim, 15–16
Berry, Chuck, 40
Berry, Halle, 90
BET (Black Entertainment Television), 50, 64,
  118, 147, 155, 160–161, 172
Beyond Demographics (study), 147
biracials, 45–47, 80–92
birther movement, 32, 34, 35
Bishop T. D. Jakes, 39, 67

Black America study, 147
Black and Green: Black Insights for the Green Movement (book), 132
Black and White Now (TV series), 43
Black Atlas, 70
Black Diaspora, 67, 77, 82, 98–92
Black Enterprise, 101, 148, 153, 155
Black Expressions (book club), 54
Black Girls Rock, Inc., 160
Black hair and identity, 42, 47–51, 90, 91–92, 156, 157–158
Black history, 8, 56, 62, 67, 77, 81, 82, 93–94, 116, 119, 137
Black is the New Green (book), 23, 121
Black Men in the Age of Obama (survey), 112, 116–117
Black Onliners, 107
Blacking Up (documentary), 39
Blogging While Black (or Brown), 13
blogs and websites
    AllHipHop.com, 173
    BlackandMarriedwithKids.com, 173
    BlackPlanet.com, 173
    BlackPlanetRadio.com, 168
    BlackWeb20.com, 173
    BlackYouthProject.com, 173
    Bossip.com, 173
    ClutchMagazine.com, 173
    Cruntastical.net, 173
    DimeWars.com, 14
    HelloBeautiful.com, 174
    JackandJillPolitics.com, 174
    KissMyBlackAds.com, 42, 46, 114, 121
    MediaTakeout.com, 174
    NecoleBitchie.com, 174
    TeachingBlackConsumers.com, 24
    SingleMAMAhood.com, 174
    StuffWhitePeopleDo (blog), 90–91
    theGrio.com, 4, 14, 34
    Vibe.com, 174
Bond, Beverly, 160
book clubs, 54–55
boomerang effect, 10, 12, 14–15
Bosley, Brad, 35
Bowen, Keith, 162
Brainwashed (book), 121
Braugher, André, 38–39
Brimm, Craig, 42, 46, 114, 121
Brockenbrough, Kevin, 58–62
Bronner, Bernard, 158

Bronson, Po, 9
Broussard, Cheryl D., 27
Buchanan, Pat, 41
Burger King, 12–13
Burgos, David, 5
Burnett, Leonard Jr., 23, 121
Burrell Communications, 58–62, 111–112, 121
Burrell, Tom, 60, 121

Cable Advertising Bureau, 121
Calhoun, Willie, 110
car sales, 52
Caribbean-born, 83–88
celebrity endorsements, 63–64
Chambers, Dr. Jason, 121
Chapman, Tracy, 7
children, 9–10, 11–12, 42–44, 122, 136–137, 179, 197
Chisholm-Mingo ad agency, 68
Christian authors, 55
Clark, Kenneth and Mamie, 43
Clear Channel Communications, 168
Clift, Robert A., 41
CNN, 9–10
Coca-Cola, 41, 192
Cole, Harriet, 154
Commonground Marketing, 172
connectors, 5, 40, 144, 161, 179, 195
Consumer Expenditure Survey, 4–5
Conversations with God (book), 166
corporal punishment, 136
Corporate Equality Index of 2010, 101
Cosby, Bill, 38
Crazy Kevin, 64
cruise vacations, 68–70
Culp, Robert, 38
cultural nuances, 94, 124–126, 184–186
cultural theft, 40–41
Cultures of Giving: Energizing and Expanding Philanthropy by and for Communities of Color (study), 118

Daniels, Lee, 101
Dargan, Elizabeth Ross, 119
Davis, Kira, 43
Davis, Naomi, 131
demographics, 1, 28, 147, 166
Derek, Bo, 41
Dexler, Jen, 7
diabetes, 72–79

dimensions of Blackness, 139–145
Dinkins, Joyce, 53
discipline, 136–137
disconnects (triggers), 40
discrimination, 8
Dis-Integration: The Splintering of Black
   America (book), 134
Diversity Affluence, 23, 65
Doubleday Direct, 54
Dyson, Michael Eric, 139–140

Ebony, 148, 153, 154–155
Echo Boomers, 10, 173
Ellis-Lamkins, Phaedra, 132
Elvis, 40
emotion, 35–40
employment in advertising, 182, 187–191
entertainment, 38–40
Essence, 50, 102, 112, 123, 138, 153, 156–157
ethnic agencies, 195
ethnic marketing and corporate culture,
   194–195

Fade2Black (video), 185
Faith Blog, 37–38
Farmer, Adam, 110
FDIC, 26
Ferguson, Mike, 110
Ford Motor, 58, 63–65
foreign-born, 80, 88–92
Fraser, George, 17, 25–26
Fullwood, Valaida, 119

Gay Pride celebrations, 98
general market, 13, 123, 144, 148, 154, 159, 164,
   189, 195
General Mills, 138–139, 179
generational divide, 10–16
GenXers, 10
Giant Foods, 81
Gibson, Mel, 38
Giving Back: A Tribute to Generations of
   African American Philanthropists (book), 119
global marketing, 92–93, 196–197
Glover, Danny, 15, 38
Glover, Jim, 122, 187–191
Go Red for Women, 177–178
Golden, Neil, 193–194
Good Hair (documentary), 48
Good Morning America, 43

Gordon, Ed, 161
Graham, Stedman, 46–47
Grainger, Ananias, 110
green movement, 130–132
Grimes, Al, 110

Hanrahan, Dan, 68
Hardy, James Earl, 100
Harris, E. Lynn, 100
Hart, Kevin, 64
Harvey, Steve, 164–165, 177, 179–180
Health, 72–79
Heart and Soul, 156–157
heart attack, 72–79
high blood pressure, 72–79
Hill, Dan, 59
Hill, Dulé, 38
Hip-Hop Generation (book), 12
Hip-Hop, xix, 12, 15, 24, 41, 121, 128, 144,
   146–147, 158, 173
Hoffman, Andrea, 23–24, 121
Honeywood, Andrew, 110
House of Payne, 3
How to Be Black (book), 121
Huffington, Arianna, 172
Hunter, John, 110

I Spy, 39
identity, xi, 8, 12, 16–17, 41–46, 139–140, 146
Identity: Passport to Freedom (book), 46–47
Ifill, Sherrilyn, 33
image, 12, 36, 37, 41, 43–46, 49, 61, 107–109,
   112, 114, 123, 161
immigrants, 2, 80–93
Indignant Generation, The (book), 56
Institute on Assets and Social Policy, 17–20
internet access, 167–168, 171–174
internet use, 120, 174, 175
Invisible Middles, 1–3, 186,
Islam, Ahmed, 172

Jackson, Alassane, 110
Jackson, Andrew, 110
Jackson, Dr. Lawrence, 56
Jackson, JoAnn, x, 66
Jackson, Phil, 110
Jackson, Jonathan, 10
Jamal, Maurice, 100–101
James, J.P., 17
Jena Six, 16

Jerry Lee Lewis, 40
Jet, 153, 154–155
Jewel-Osco, 81
Johnson Publishing, 154
Johnson, Sheila, 172
Johnson-Rice, Linda, 154
Jones Magazine, 153
Jones, Sandra, 138
Jones, Van, 132
Journal of Marriage and Family, 9
journalism, 35–36
Joyner, Tom, 69, 76, 111, 117, 164, 165

K&G Fashion Superstore, 180
Kemp, Herb, v, xii, 2–3, 172
Kensey and Kensey Communications, 55
Kensey, Barbara, 55–56
King, Tim, 110
Kitwana, Bakari, 12
Knowles, Beyoncé, 44

language, xv, 5–6, 81–82, 85, 87, 167
Latinos, xii, 1, 5–6, 80, 83–88, 167, 172, 183, 185
Lattimer Communications, 122–127, 147
Lemon, Don, 102
Lethal Weapon, 38
LGBTs, 2, 97–106, 271, 185
Life Outside the Box, (study), 97
Little Richard, 40
Logo (cable channel), 100
Long, Nia, 15, 154
Los Angeles Sentinel (newspaper), 152
Lowe, Mira, 154
lower-income households, xiv, 18–20, 21, 93
Lucas, Wonya, 162

Mackey, Carol, 54
Mad Man (book), 187–188
Madison Avenue and the Color Line (book), 121
Madison Avenue Initiative, 191
Madison Avenue Project, 188
magazine engagement, 159
Magic Johnson, 180
Mahoney, Tim, 64
Major Blackard, 33
Marcus Graham Project, 189
market research, xv, 92, 97, 161, 182–186
marketing budget, 12, 27–28
Marketing to the New Majority, (book), 5
Maxwell, John C., 198

Mayo, Barry, 168
Mazzarino, Jim, 42–43
McDonald's Corporation, 137–138, 192, 193–194, 196
McMillan, Terry, 54–54
McNally, Deborah, 23–24
Meet the Browns, 3
Meeting David Wilson, (documentary), 14
men, 36, 38–39, 40, 60–61106–113, 114, 141–143
Men of a Certain Age (TV show), 38–39
middle class, 72, 140, 142, 174, 17,
Millennial Men (chart), 144
Millennials, xi, 10–14, 15–16, 116, 141
Miller, Brandon, 110
Miller, Mary, 109
Miller, Ronald, 110
Millward Brown, 5–6
ministers, 37–38
Ministry Marketing Solutions, 55
mixed race marriages, 90
mobile phone use, 22, 167–168
Mobolade, Ola, 5
Mocha Moms, 14
Monday, Curtis R., 110
Mooz-Lum (film), 15
Mora, Ebele, 171
Morse, David, 103n, 185–186
Moss, Rev. Otis III, 110
Mowry-Hardrict,Tia, 161
MSNBC, 14
Muléy, Miriam, 121
MultiCultClassics (blog), 56
Muppet, 42
Muslim, 13–14
My Black is Beautiful, 44–45, 49–50

NAACP, 33, 91, 102, 117, 119, 162
National Public Radio, 118, 140
National Urban League, 17, 91, 119
Nelson, Neil, 14
New American Dimensions, 103n, 185–186
New Hope Publishers, 53
Newman-Carrasco, Rachel, 7–8
Nielsen, 2, 174
Noah's Arc, 100
North Paran, 54–55
NurtureShock (book), 9

O.J. Simpson trial, 31
O'Brien, Soledad, 108

Obama, Barack, xii, 30–34, 36, 112, 117, 171
Obama, Michelle, 77
Ollarvia, Clayton and LaNise, 108–109
one-drop concept, 80, 89–90
Our Weekly (newspaper), 150
Out & Equal Workplace Advocates, 101

Padron, Alberto, 84–85
Patton, Erin O., 121
PepsiCo, 35–36
Perry, Marc, 63
Perry, Pam, 55
Perry, Ravi, 102
Perry, Tyler, 1–3, 4, 103
Pettus, Ted, 121
Pew Research, 150, 167
philanthropy, 54, 118–119
Pine-Sol, 127–128
Polk, Patrik-Ian, 100
Poniewozik, James, 162
post-Civil Rights, 8, 30, 115, 116, 136, 148
post-racial society, 9, 10–14, 121, 141
Potter's House, 67
Power To End Stroke, 176–178
pre-Civil Rights, 12, 30, 115, 136
Prince, Richard, 150
Procter & Gamble, 192–193, 49–50
progressive thinking, 6–8
Pryor, Richard, 38
Psych, 38
Publix, 81, 96–97

Quinlan, Mary Lou, 6–7

R.L. Polk, 58, 65
racial wealth gap, 17–19
radio listening trends, 117, 152, 163–169
Radio One, 147, 163–164, 166, 167–168
Radio One Black America Study, 12, 147
Real Men Charities, 111
Real Times Media, 151
Recession, 17
Reid, Iziah, 14
religion, 37–38, 165–167
respect, xv, 8, 30, 31, 34, 40, 41, 109, 117, 133, 134–138, 171
Rev. Dr. Jeremiah Wright, 37
Rev. Martin Luther King, Jr., ix, 33–34, 111
Rhett, Pamela, 49
Roberts, Cynthia Roberts, 121

Robinson, Eugene, 134
Rock, Chris, 48–49
Rockefeller Philanthropy Advisors, 118
Rod 2.0, 99
Roday, James, 38
Rodriguez, Robert, PhD, 194
Rogers, Desireé, 154
Rolling Out (newspaper), 152
Romano, Ray, 38
romantic love, 36–37, 40, 114, 144, 162
Royal Caribbean Cruise Lines, 68–69
Ruth C. Hunter African-American Market
    Research Scholarship, 184

Sanders, Brad, 110
Saturday Night Live, 31
Schildkret, Alex, 150
segmentation by race, 7, 140, 147
Seitsinger, Sean, 19
self-esteem, 8
Sharpton, Rev. Al, 117, 191
Shelley, Dan, 167
Sheridan Gospel Network (SGN), 166
Sheridan, Will, 102
Silent Generation, 10
Silva, Helda M., 151
skin color, 9, 43–44, 45–47
slavery, 8, 38, 41, 82, 90, 109
Smiley, Tavis, 117
Smith, Bev, 117
SMSi, 138, 179–180
social media, 32, 63–64, 144–145, 149, 156, 170–175, 176–178
Society Pages, 106
Sophisticate's Black Hair, 157–158
Soul Train, 148
South Florida Times (newspaper), 150–151
spending power, 4, 17–20
Star Trek, 35
Starcom Media, 147
State of Black America Report, 19
Steed Media Group, 152
Steed, Munson, 152, 191
Stephens, Lincoln, 189
Step-Off Competition, 41
Stevens, Jay, 164
Stinson, Denise, 55
Stir Crazy, 38
Strategic Visions, 57
stroke, 79, 176–177

"Summertime" (song), 57
Sykes, Wanda, 102
Symphony IRI, 20

Target Market News, 4, 28n, 71n, 113n, 181n, 191n
targeted media, 148–149
Tate, Jeffrey, 189
Taylor, Goldie, 33
Taylor, Susan L., 179
Tea Party, 15, 31–32
The 2010 Lower-Income Multicultural Shopper Study, 18–19
The 85% Niche, 121
The Africa Channel, 163
The Black Star Project, 110
The Break Up (film), 133–134
The Chicago Defender (newspaper), 151
The Game, 90, 161–162, 172
The John Maxwell Daily Reader, 198
The MOSES Movement, 25–26
The Rachel Maddow Show, 41
The Selig Center for Economic Growth, 4
The State of Black Women, 2010, 123
The State of the African-American Consumer (report), 174
The Yolanda Adams Morning Show, 166
Thistlethwaite, Susan Brooks, 37–38
Thomas, Charles, 119
Thompson, Dana, 21–23
Thurston, Baratunde, 121, 170–171
Tide with Downey, 112
Tita-Reid, Najoh, 44, 49–50
Touré, 45–46, 73, 121, 139–140
Toyota, 58–62
Transcendent Elite, 140
travel, 23, 52, 65–70, 142, 175
Trice-Edney News Wire Service, 151
Trice-Edney, Hazel, 151
trichtomous identity, 86–93
Trinity UCC, 67
TrueStar Magazine, 158
Trump, Donald, 32–36
TUV Mediaworks, 171
TV One, 64, 144, 155, 160, 162

Under the Influence: Tracing the Hip-Hop Generation's Impact on Brands, Sports, and Pop Culture, 121
underground economy, 18
unemployment rate, 18
United Lesbians of African Heritage, 99
Uniworld, 63
Upscale, 158
Uptown Magazine, 153
Uptown Media, 24
Urban Prep Academies, 110

values, 57, 59, 92, 147, 161, 166
Vibe Lifestyle Network, 23
Vokes, Amy, 154–165

W.K. Kellogg Foundation, 118
Walsch, Neal Donald, 168
Washington Post, 37–38, 134
Watkins, S. Craig, 167
Webber, Harry, 188
Wells Fargo, 102
What She's Not Telling You (book), 6–7
Who's Afraid of Post-Blackness? What It Means to Be Black Now (book) 45–46, 73, 121, 139–140
Wilder, Gene, 38
Will Smith, 57
Williams, Carol H., 188, 192
Williams, Kelly, 174
Williams, Kisha Mitchell, 49
Wilson, David A., 4, 14
Wilson, Greg, 110
Woodard, Larry, 133
women, 7, 14, 44–45, 112, 122–128, 147, 156, 160, 164, 173, 174, 178–179, 186, 198
Worell, Marti, 36–37
WVON (radio station), 117

XXL, 158

Yankelovich, 136, 149
youth, 10, 12, 144, 146–147, 152, 158, 171, 173

Zeta Tau Alpha, 41